California Cable Car

Take a ride on a trolley car and see the sights! Find out more about living in California at:
www.harcourtschool.com/hss

Reflections

CALIFORNIA SERIES

A Child's View

Harcourt
SCHOOL PUBLISHERS

Orlando   Austin   New York   San Diego   Toronto   London
Visit *The Learning Site!* www.harcourtschool.com

MAPQUEST

TIME
FOR KIDS

Reflections

A CHILD'S VIEW

Senior Author

Dr. Priscilla H. Porter
Professor Emeritus
School of Education
California State University, Dominguez Hills
Center for History–Social Science Education
Carson, California

Series Authors

Dr. Michael J. Berson
Associate Professor
Social Science Education
University of South Florida
Tampa, Florida

Dr. Margaret Hill
History–Social Science Coordinator
San Bernardino County Superintendent of Schools
Director, Schools of California Online Resources for
   Education: History–Social Science
San Bernardino, California

Dr. Tyrone C. Howard
Assistant Professor
UCLA Graduate School of Education & Information Studies
University of California at Los Angeles
Los Angeles, California

Dr. Bruce E. Larson
Associate Professor
Social Science Education/Secondary Education
Woodring College of Education
Western Washington University
Bellingham, Washington

Dr. Julio Moreno
Assistant Professor
Department of History
University of San Francisco
San Francisco, California

Series Consultants

Martha Berner
Consulting Teacher
Cajon Valley Union School District
San Diego County, California

Dr. James Charkins
Professor of Economics
California State University
San Bernardino, California
Executive Director of California Council on Economic
   Education

Rhoda Coleman
K–12 Reading Consultant Lecturer
California State University, Dominguez Hills
Carson, California

Dr. Robert Kumamoto
Professor
History Department
San Jose State University
San Jose, California

Carlos Lossada
Co-Director Professional Development Specialist
UCLA History–Geography Project
University of California, Los Angeles
Regional Coordinator, California Geographic Alliance
Los Angeles, California

Dr. Tanis Thorne
Director of Native Studies
Lecturer in History
Department of History
University of California, Irvine
Irvine, California

Rebecca Valbuena
Los Angeles County Teacher of the Year—2004–05
Language Development Specialist
Stanton Elementary School
Glendora Unified School District
Glendora, California

Dr. Phillip VanFossen
Associate Professor, Social Studies Education
Associate Director, Purdue Center for Economic Education
Department of Curriculum
Purdue University
West Lafayette, Indiana

Content Reviewer

Dr. Judson Grenier
Professor of History Emeritus
California State University, Dominguez Hills
Carson, California

Classroom Reviewers and Contributors

Staci Andrews
Teacher
Delevan Drive Elementary School
Los Angeles, California

Kristin Carver
Teacher
Fairmount Elementary School
San Francisco, California

Susan Christenson
Teacher
McKinley Elementary School
San Gabriel, California

Fifi Chu
Teacher
Repetto Elementary School
Monterey Park, California

Linda Dean
Teacher
Webster School
Fresno, California

Stacey Firpo
Teacher
Aynesworth Elementary School
Fresno, California

Gay Grieger-Lods
Teacher
Wilson School
Richmond, California

Kathleen L. Hovore
Teacher
North Park Elementary School
Valencia, California

Kathy Stendel
Teacher
North Park Elementary School
Valencia, California

Harcourt
SCHOOL PUBLISHERS

Maps
researched and prepared by

MAPQUEST.COM

Readers
written and designed by

TIME FOR KIDS

Copyright © 2007 by Harcourt, Inc.

All rights reserved. No part of this publication may be reproduced or transmitted in any form or by any means, electronic or mechanical, including photocopy, recording, or any information storage and retrieval system, without permission in writing from the publisher.

Requests for permission to make copies of any part of the work should be mailed to:

School Permissions and Copyrights
Harcourt, Inc.
6277 Sea Harbor Drive
Orlando, Florida 32887-6777
Fax: 407-345-2418

REFLECTIONS is a trademark of Harcourt, Inc. HARCOURT and the Harcourt Logos are trademarks of Harcourt, Inc., registered in the United States of America and/or other jurisdictions. TIME FOR KIDS and the red border are registered trademarks of Time Inc. Used under license. Copyright © by Time Inc. All rights reserved.

Acknowledgments appear in the back of this book.

Printed in the United States of America

ISBN 0-15-338498-0

2 3 4 5 6 7 8 9 10 032 15 14 13 12 11 10 09 08 07 06 05

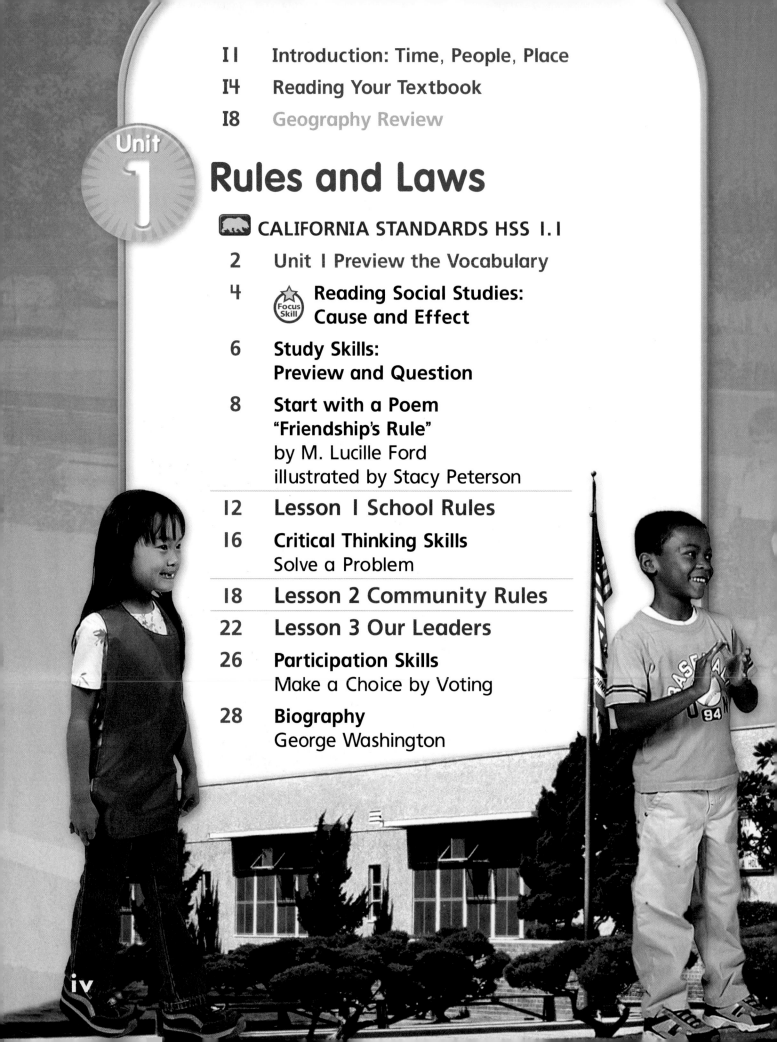

11   Introduction: Time, People, Place

14   Reading Your Textbook

18   Geography Review

Unit
1

Rules and Laws

🐻 CALIFORNIA STANDARDS HSS 1.1

2   Unit 1 Preview the Vocabulary

4   (Focus Skill) **Reading Social Studies: Cause and Effect**

6   **Study Skills: Preview and Question**

8   **Start with a Poem** "Friendship's Rule" by M. Lucille Ford illustrated by Stacy Peterson

12   **Lesson 1 School Rules**

16   **Critical Thinking Skills** Solve a Problem

18   **Lesson 2 Community Rules**

22   **Lesson 3 Our Leaders**

26   **Participation Skills** Make a Choice by Voting

28   **Biography** George Washington

iv

30 **Lesson 4 The Golden Rule**

34 **Participation Skills**
Work and Play Together

36 **Citizenship**
Police Officers and You

38 **End with a Play**
The Lion and the Mouse
by Aesop
illustrated by David Diaz

42 **Field Trip**
The Capitol

44 **Unit 1 Review**

48 **Unit 1 Activities**

Unit 2

Where People Live

CALIFORNIA STANDARDS HSS 1.2

50 Unit 2 Preview the Vocabulary

52 **Reading Social Studies:
    Categorize and Classify**

54 **Study Skills:
    Build Vocabulary**

56 **Start with a Poem
    "Making Maps"**
    by Elaine V. Emans
    illustrated by Rob Dunlavey

58 **Lesson 1 Finding Where You Are**

62 **Map and Globe Skills**
    Use a Globe

64 **Lesson 2 Neighborhood Map**

68 **Map and Globe Skills**
    Read a Map

vi

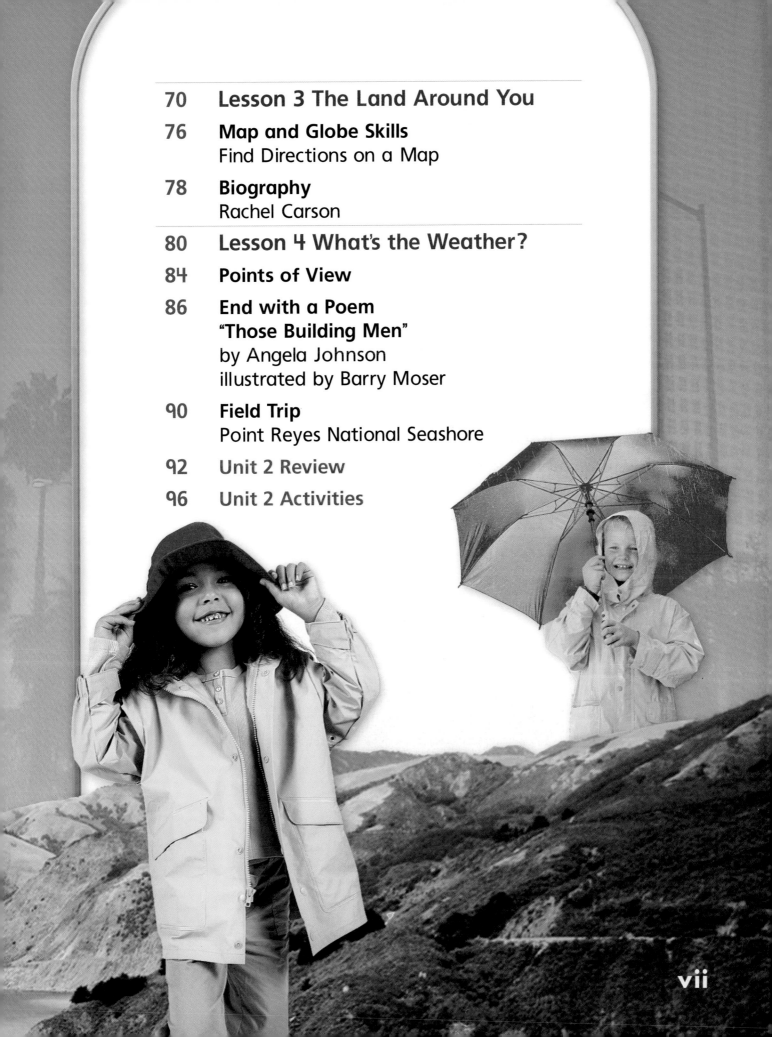

70   **Lesson 3 The Land Around You**

76   **Map and Globe Skills**
Find Directions on a Map

78   **Biography**
Rachel Carson

80   **Lesson 4 What's the Weather?**

84   **Points of View**

86   **End with a Poem**
"Those Building Men"
by Angela Johnson
illustrated by Barry Moser

90   **Field Trip**
Point Reyes National Seashore

92   **Unit 2 Review**

96   **Unit 2 Activities**

Unit 3

We Love Our Country

CALIFORNIA STANDARDS HSS 1.3

98   Unit 3 Preview the Vocabulary

100   **Reading Social Studies:** Main Idea and Details

102   **Study Skills:** Note Taking

104   **Start with a Song** **"America"** by Samuel F. Smith illustrated by Erika LeBarre

106   **Lesson 1 I Pledge Allegiance**

110   **Biography** Francis Bellamy

112   **Lesson 2 Heroes and Holidays**

116   **Chart and Graph Skills** Read a Calendar

118   **Citizenship** Flag Day

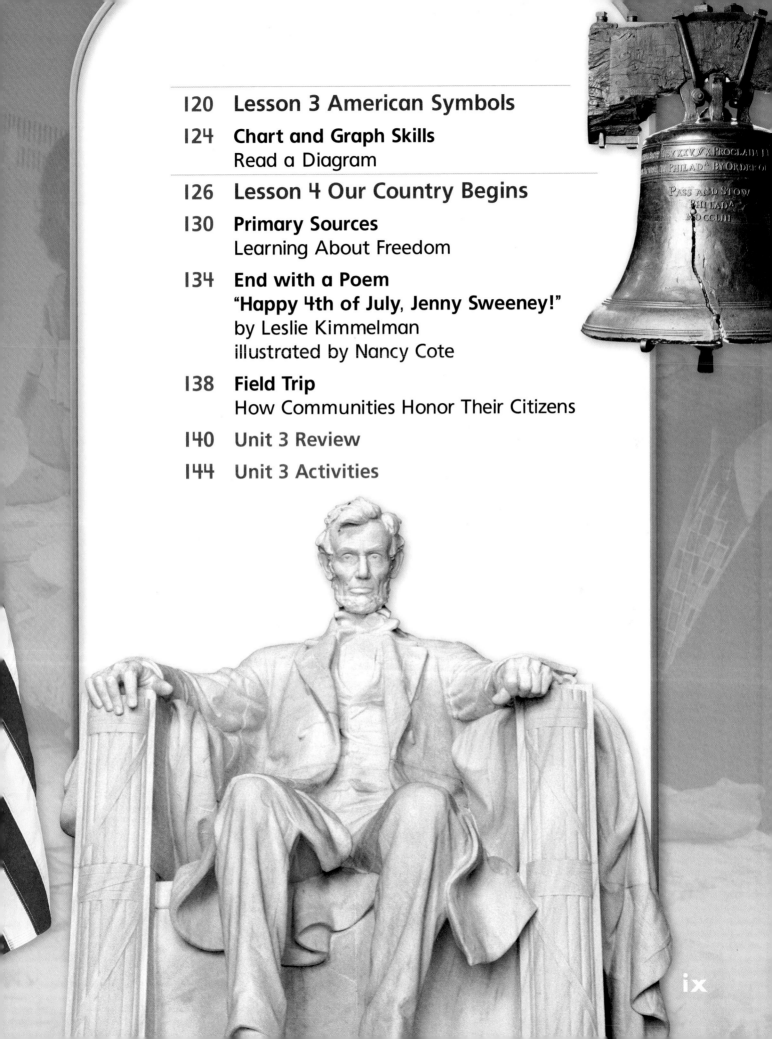

120 **Lesson 3 American Symbols**

124 **Chart and Graph Skills**
Read a Diagram

126 **Lesson 4 Our Country Begins**

130 **Primary Sources**
Learning About Freedom

134 **End with a Poem**
"Happy 4th of July, Jenny Sweeney!"
by Leslie Kimmelman
illustrated by Nancy Cote

138 **Field Trip**
How Communities Honor Their Citizens

140 **Unit 3 Review**

144 **Unit 3 Activities**

Unit 4

Our Changing World

🐻 CALIFORNIA STANDARDS HSS 1.4

146 Unit 4 Preview the Vocabulary

148 ⭐Focus Skill **Reading Social Studies:**
Sequence

150 **Study Skills:**
Use Visuals

152 **Start with a Poem**
"Children of Long Ago"
by Lessie Jones Little
illustrated by Jan Spivey Gilchrist

158 **Lesson 1 Schools Long Ago**

164 **Chart and Graph Skills**
Put Things in Groups

166 **Lesson 2 Communities in the Past**

170 **Chart and Graph Skills**
Use a Time Line

172 **Citizenship**
Learning Through Storytelling

x

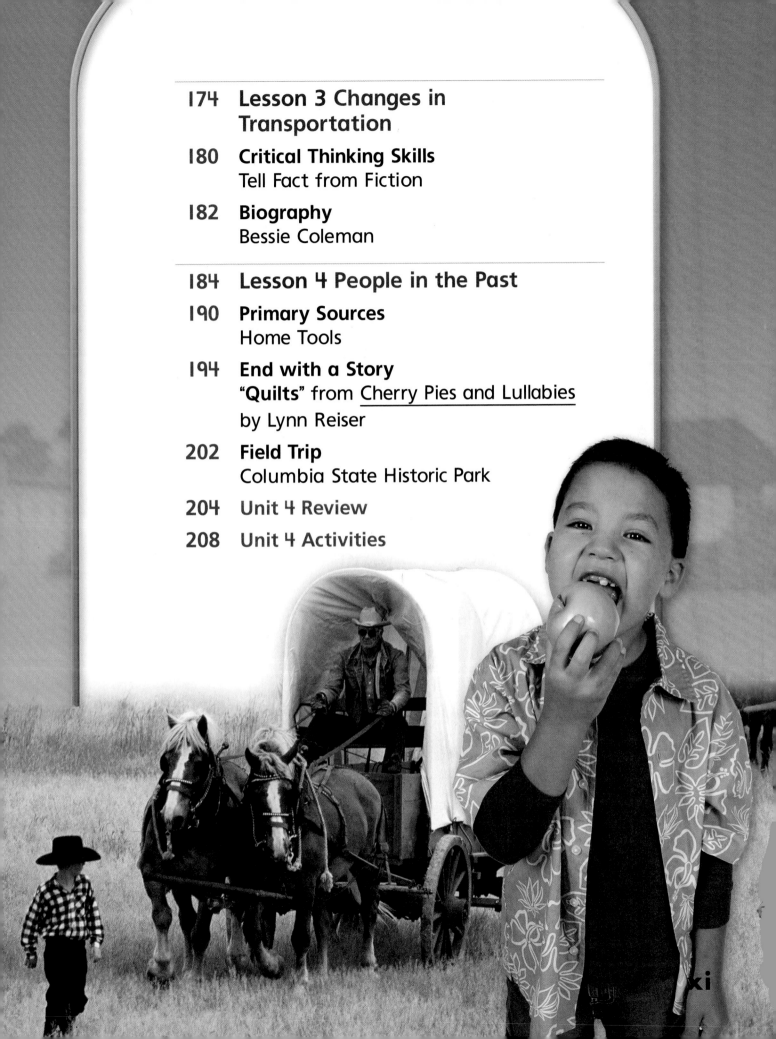

174 **Lesson 3 Changes in Transportation**

180 **Critical Thinking Skills**
Tell Fact from Fiction

182 **Biography**
Bessie Coleman

184 **Lesson 4 People in the Past**

190 **Primary Sources**
Home Tools

194 **End with a Story**
"**Quilts**" from Cherry Pies and Lullabies
by Lynn Reiser

202 **Field Trip**
Columbia State Historic Park

204 **Unit 4 Review**

208 **Unit 4 Activities**

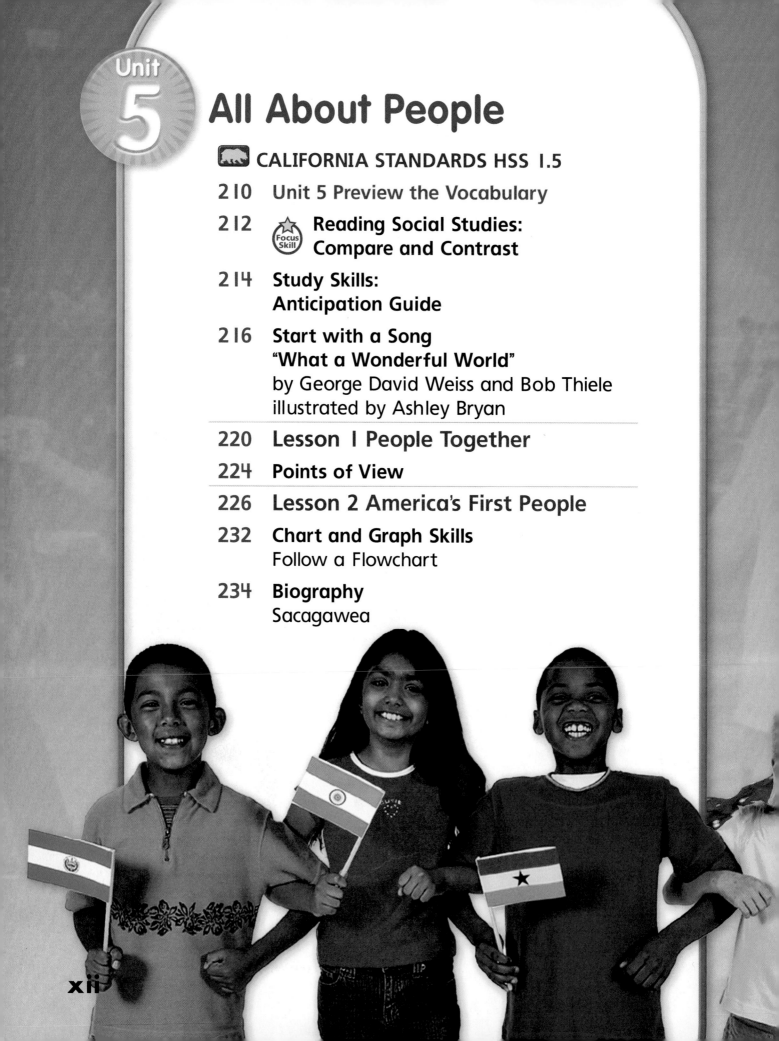

Unit 5

All About People

CALIFORNIA STANDARDS HSS 1.5

210   Unit 5 Preview the Vocabulary

212   **Reading Social Studies:**
      Compare and Contrast

214   **Study Skills:**
      Anticipation Guide

216   **Start with a Song**
      "What a Wonderful World"
      by George David Weiss and Bob Thiele
      illustrated by Ashley Bryan

220   **Lesson 1 People Together**

224   **Points of View**

226   **Lesson 2 America's First People**

232   **Chart and Graph Skills**
      Follow a Flowchart

234   **Biography**
      Sacagawea

236 **Lesson 3 People Find New Homes**

242 **Map and Globe Skills**
Follow a Route

244 **Lesson 4 Expressing Culture**

250 **Lesson 5 Sharing Cultures**

254 **End with a Folktale**
"How Beetles Became Beautiful"
illustrated by Christopher Corr

258 **Field Trip**
International Festival of Masks

260 **Unit 5 Review**

264 **Unit 5 Activities**

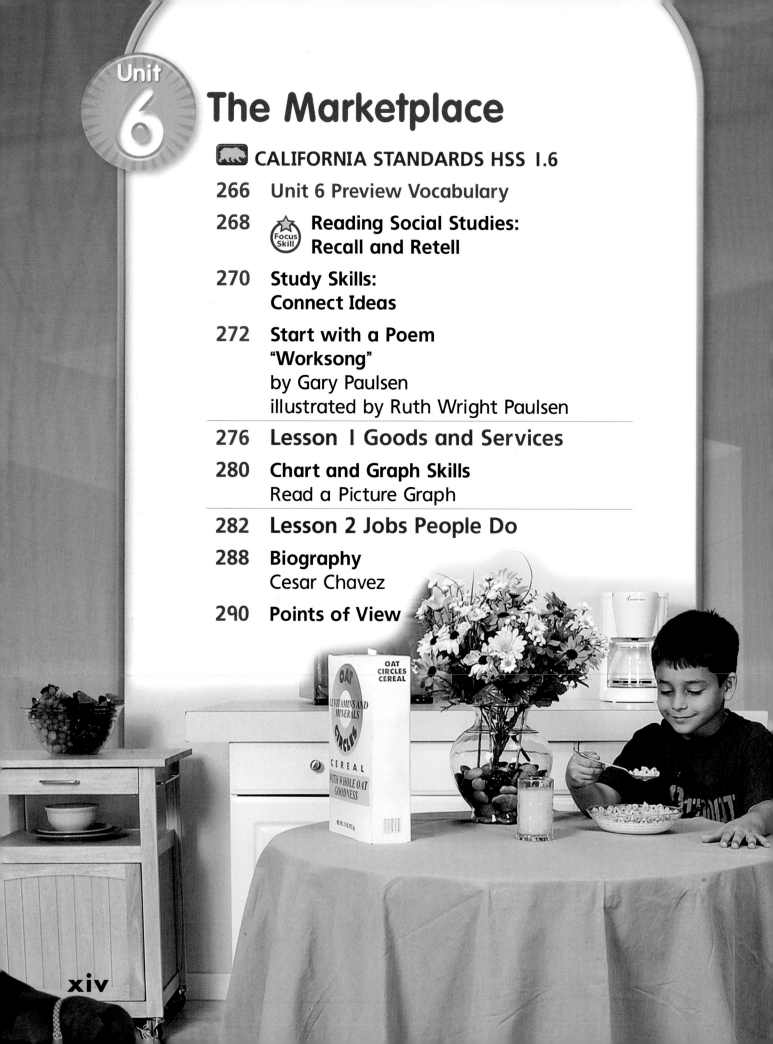

Unit 6

The Marketplace

CALIFORNIA STANDARDS HSS 1.6

266 Unit 6 Preview Vocabulary

268 Focus Skill **Reading Social Studies: Recall and Retell**

270 **Study Skills: Connect Ideas**

272 **Start with a Poem "Worksong"** by Gary Paulsen illustrated by Ruth Wright Paulsen

276 **Lesson 1 Goods and Services**

280 **Chart and Graph Skills** Read a Picture Graph

282 **Lesson 2 Jobs People Do**

288 **Biography** Cesar Chavez

290 **Points of View**

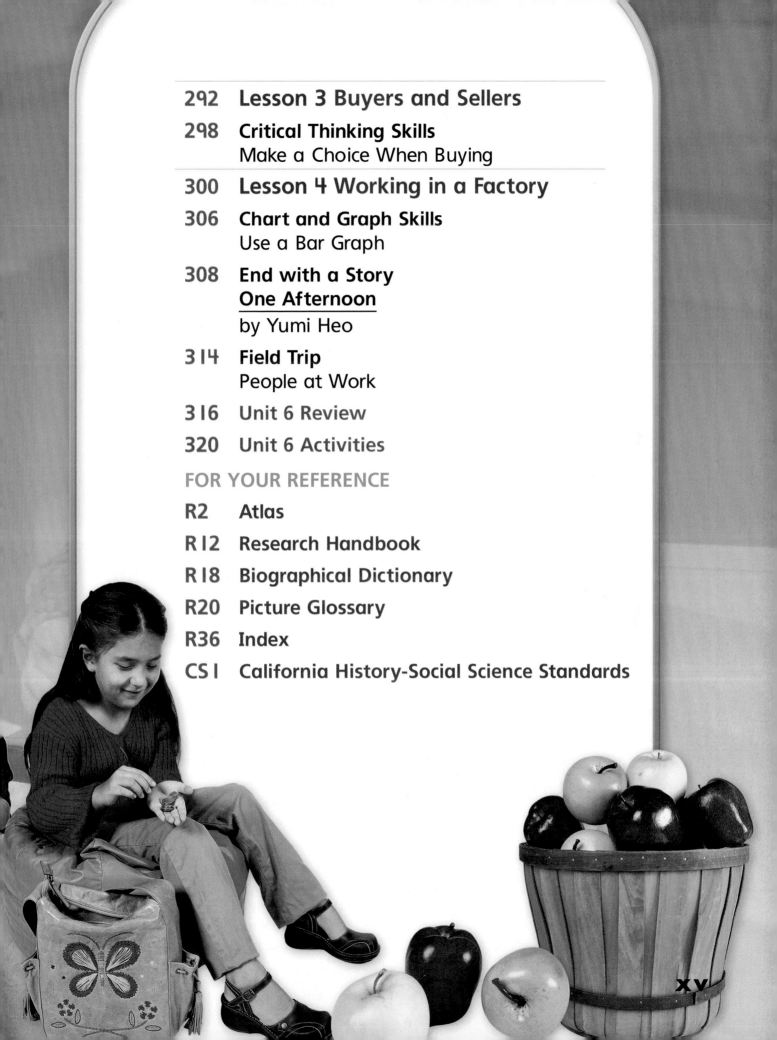

292 **Lesson 3 Buyers and Sellers**

298 **Critical Thinking Skills**
Make a Choice When Buying

300 **Lesson 4 Working in a Factory**

306 **Chart and Graph Skills**
Use a Bar Graph

308 **End with a Story**
One Afternoon
by Yumi Heo

314 **Field Trip**
People at Work

316 **Unit 6 Review**

320 **Unit 6 Activities**

FOR YOUR REFERENCE

R2 **Atlas**

R12 **Research Handbook**

R18 **Biographical Dictionary**

R20 **Picture Glossary**

R36 **Index**

CS1 **California History-Social Science Standards**

Features

Skills

Chart and Graph Skills

116 Read a Calendar
124 Read a Diagram
164 Put Things in Groups
170 Use a Time Line
232 Follow a Flowchart
280 Read a Picture Graph
306 Use a Bar Graph

Participation Skills

26 Make a Choice by Voting
34 Work and Play Together

Map and Globe Skills

62 Use a Globe
68 Read a Map
76 Find Directions on a Map
242 Follow a Route

Critical Thinking Skills

16 Solve a Problem
180 Tell Fact from Fiction
298 Make a Choice When Buying

Reading Social Studies

4 Cause and Effect
52 Categorize and Classify
100 Main Idea and Details
148 Sequence
212 Compare and Contrast
268 Recall and Retell

Study Skills

6 Preview and Question
54 Build Vocabulary
102 Note Taking
150 Use Visuals
214 Anticipation Guide
270 Connect Ideas

Citizenship

36 Police Officers and You
118 Flag Day
172 Learning Through Storytelling

Points of View

84 Where You Live
224 Cultures in Your Community
290 Important Jobs

Literature and Music

8 "Friendship's Rule"
by M. Lucille Ford
illustrated by Stacy Peterson

38 The Lion and the Mouse
by Aesop
illustrated by David Diaz

56 "Making Maps"
by Elaine V. Emans
illustrated by Rob Dunlavey

86 "Those Building Men"
by Angela Johnson
illustrated by Barry Moser

104 "America"
by Samuel F. Smith
illustrated by Erika LeBarre

134 "Happy 4th of July, Jenny Sweeney!"
by Leslie Kimmelman
illustrated by Nancy Cote

152 "Children of Long Ago"
    by Lessie Jones Little
    illustrated by Jan Spivey Gilchrist
194 "Quilts" from Cherry Pies and Lullabies
    by Lynn Reiser
216 "What a Wonderful World"
    by George David Weiss and Bob Thiele
    illustrated by Ashley Bryan
254 "How Beetles Became Beautiful"
    illustrated by Christopher Corr
272 "Worksong"
    by Gary Paulsen
    illustrated by Ruth Wright Paulsen
308 One Afternoon
    by Yumi Heo

Primary Sources

130 Learning About Freedom
190 Home Tools

Documents

130 Page from John Adams's Journal
132 The Declaration of Independence
133 The United States Constitution
183 Bessie Coleman's Pilot's License

Biography

 28 George Washington
 78 Rachel Carson
110 Francis Bellamy
182 Bessie Coleman
234 Sacagawea
288 Cesar Chavez

Geography

 24 Sacramento
127 The 13 Colonies

Cultural Heritage

 31 Confucius
 74 Adobe Houses
239 German Immigrants

Children in History

123 Moving to America
162 George S. Parker
285 Addie Laird

A Closer Look

161 School Tools of Long Ago
295 How Money Moves

Field Trips

 42 The Capitol
 90 Point Reyes National Seashore
138 How Communities Honor Their Citizens
202 Columbia State Historic Park
258 International Festival of Masks
314 People at Work

Charts, Graphs, and Diagrams

  5 Cause and Effect
  7 K-W-L Chart
 26 Ballot
 27 Vote Tally Chart
 46 Problem-Solutions Chart
 47 Votes for a Class Pet
 53 Categorize and Classify
 55 Word Web
 73 Ways We Use Land and Water
101 Main Idea and Details
103 Learning Log
117 February Calendar

125 The Statue of Liberty
142 January Calendar
143 United States Capitol
149 Sequence
165 School Tools
206 Transportation
213 Compare and Contrast
215 Anticipation Guide
233 How the Chumash Indians Made Acorn Soup
263 How to Make a Chinese Lantern
269 Recall and Retell
271 Flowchart
281 Baskets of Apples Sold
295 How Money Moves
307 Boxes of Crayons Sold
318 Mr. Wilson's Toy Store
319 Mr. Wheel's Car Repair Services

127 The 13 Colonies
131 The 13 Colonies, 1775
138 Big Sur, Santa Ana, and Riverside
202 Columbia
226 American Indian Tribes
230 California Indian Crafts
243 San Francisco to Blythe
258 Los Angeles
262 Eureka to San Jose
R2 World Continents
R4 World Land and Water
R6 United States States and Capitals
R8 United States Land and Water
R10 California Cities and Towns
R11 California Land and Water

Maps

24 Sacramento
42 Sacramento
50 Map of California
58 Community Map
59 Cities in California
60 United States
61 California
63 Western Hemisphere
63 Eastern Hemisphere
69 Neighborhood
77 School Map
90 Point Reyes
94 My Neighborhood
95 Zoo
126 The Mayflower

Time Lines

29 George Washington Time Line
79 Rachel Carson Time Line
111 Francis Bellamy Time Line
170 Marc's Time Line
183 Bessie Coleman Time Line
207 Mary's Time Line
235 Sacagawea Time Line
289 Cesar Chavez Time Line

The Story Well Told

"America! America!
God shed his grace on thee
And crown thy good with brotherhood
From sea to shining sea!"

"America the Beautiful" by Katharine Lee Bates

Do you ever wonder about your world? This year you will be learning how our country has grown over **time**. You will read about the **people** in your world and how they get along. Also, you will compare the ways people live in many different **places**.

Time People Place

A Child's View

You can learn more about yourself by looking at people who lived before you.

Americans share many ideas.

Your view of the world may depend on where you live.

Reading Your Textbook

GETTING STARTED

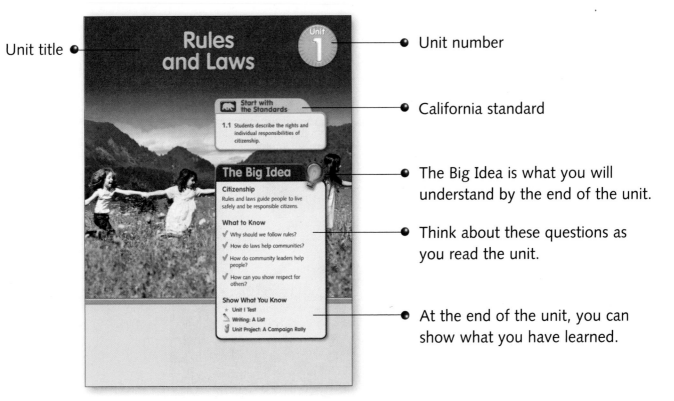

Unit title

Unit number

California standard

The Big Idea is what you will understand by the end of the unit.

Think about these questions as you read the unit.

At the end of the unit, you can show what you have learned.

PREVIEW VOCABULARY

The photograph helps you understand the meaning of the word.

The definition tells you what the word means. The page number tells you where to find the word in this unit.

The unit has more information and activities on the website.

Each new word is highlighted in yellow.

READING SOCIAL STUDIES

Reading skill and explanation

Model paragraph for reading practice

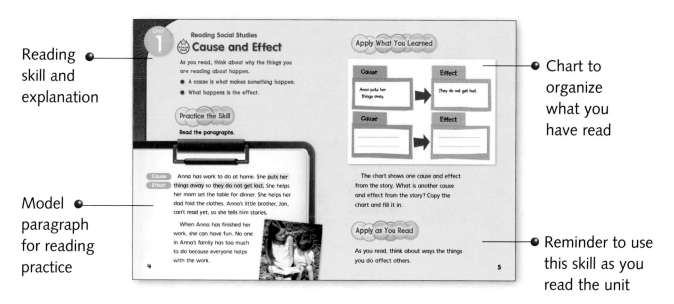

Chart to organize what you have read

Reminder to use this skill as you read the unit

STUDY SKILLS

Study skill and explanation

Activity to practice study skill

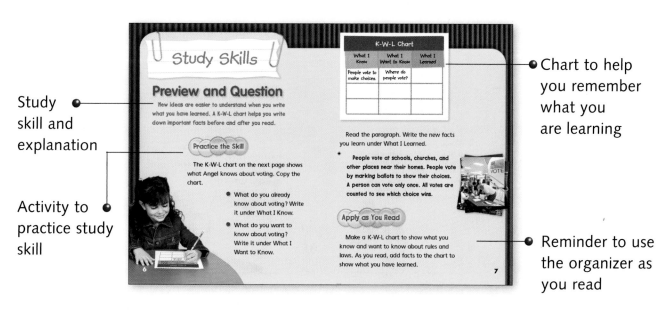

Chart to help you remember what you are learning

Reminder to use the organizer as you read

READING A LESSON

Lesson number

Guiding question

Some main ideas to find

New words to learn

Reminder to use your reading skill

California standards

Lesson title

Summary of the lesson

Questions and activities to check what you have learned

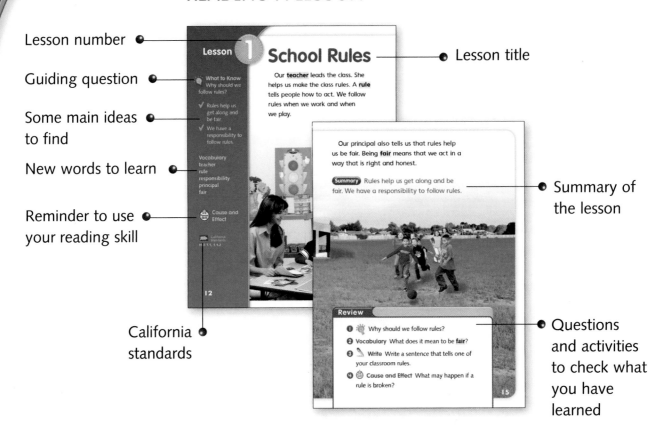

PRACTICING SKILLS

Skill lessons help you build your map and globe, chart and graph, critical thinking, and participation skills.

Skill category

Skill lesson title

Why the skill is important

Skill practice questions

Independent skill practice activity

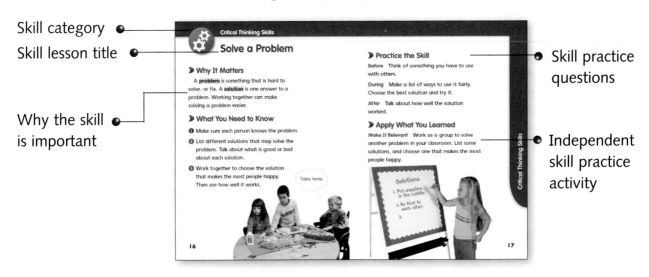

SPECIAL FEATURES

Every unit starts and ends with a story, play, poem, song, article, or folktale.

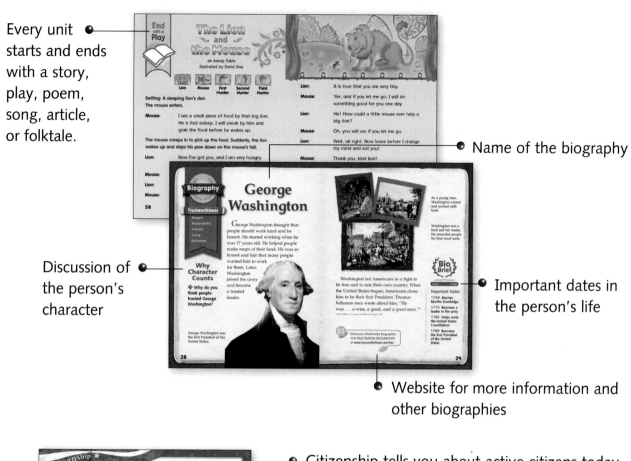

Name of the biography

Discussion of the person's character

Important dates in the person's life

Website for more information and other biographies

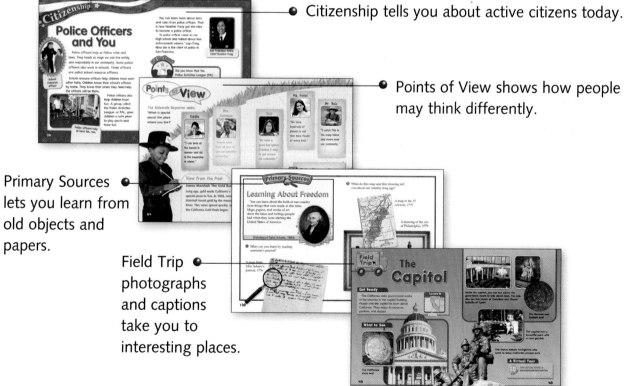

Citizenship tells you about active citizens today.

Points of View shows how people may think differently.

Primary Sources lets you learn from old objects and papers.

Field Trip photographs and captions take you to interesting places.

Go to the Reference section in the back of this book to see other special features.

The Five Themes of Geography

The story of people is also the story of where they live. When scientists talk about Earth, they think about five themes or main ideas.

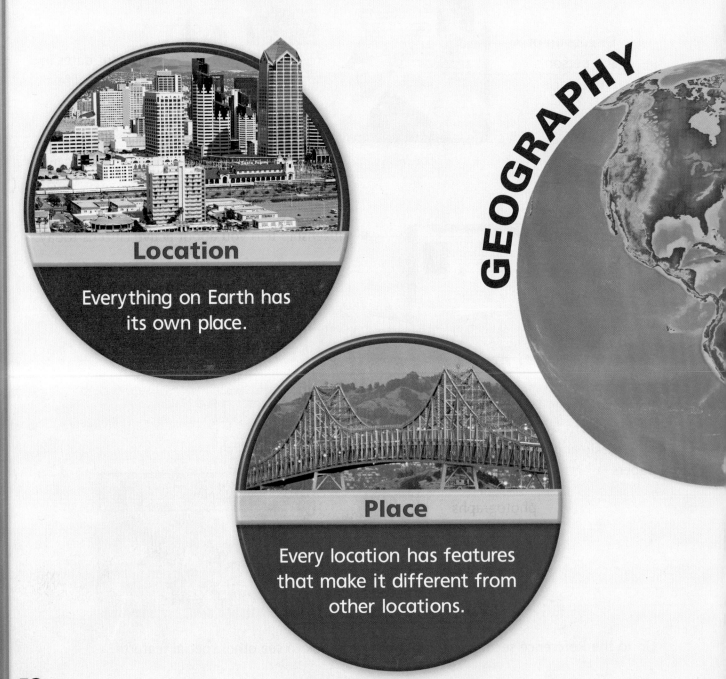

GEOGRAPHY

Location

Everything on Earth has its own place.

Place

Every location has features that make it different from other locations.

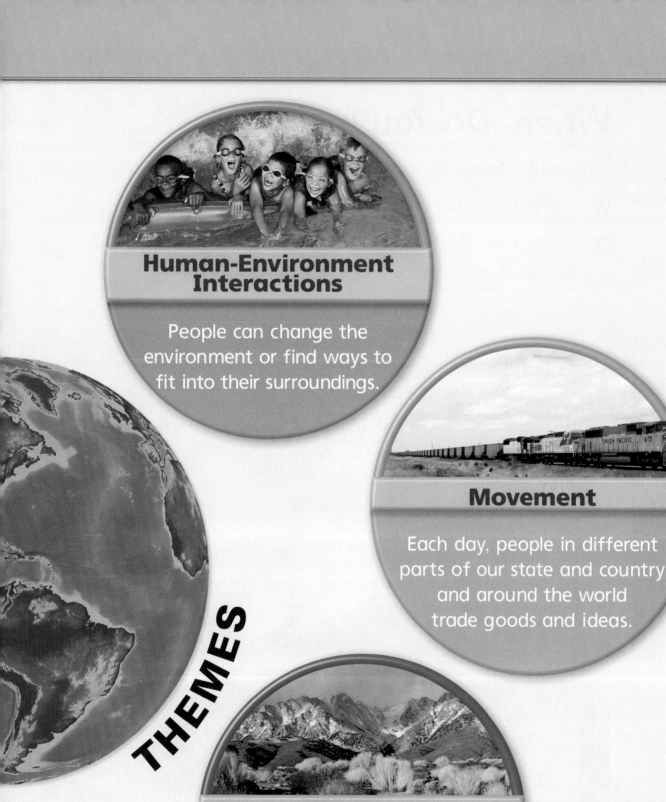

Human-Environment Interactions

People can change the environment or find ways to fit into their surroundings.

Movement

Each day, people in different parts of our state and country and around the world trade goods and ideas.

THEMES

Regions

Areas of Earth that share features that make them different from other areas are called regions.

Where Do You Live?

Families have addresses. An **address** tells where people live. It has a number and a street name. Read Pedro's address.

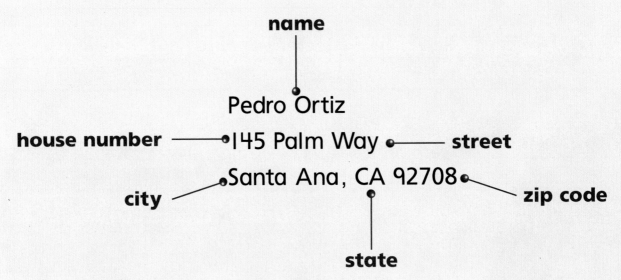

name

Pedro Ortiz

house number ——— 145 Palm Way ●— street

city ——— Santa Ana, CA 92708 ●——— zip code

state

Home Address

ANALYSIS SKILL Look at the map. Find Pedro's house. What is the number of his neighbor's house across the street?

Where Are You?

Look at the drawing of a school from above. It shows where the rooms are in a school. Describe where each room is located. Use words such as **next to**, **beside**, and **across from**.

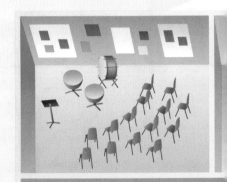

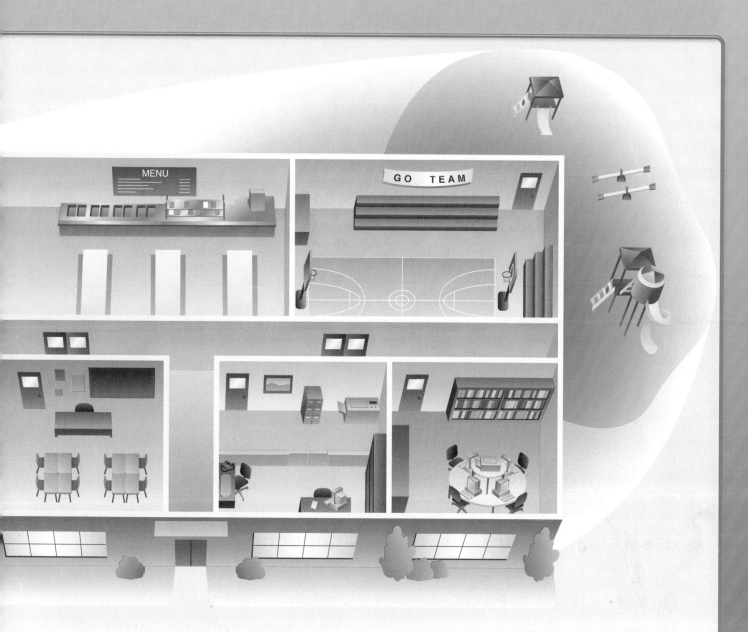

1 How is this school like your school?

2 Imagine you are helping a child who is new to your school. Describe how to get to the rooms he or she might need to find.

desert a large, dry area of land

forest a large area of trees

gulf a large body of ocean water that is partly surrounded by land

hill land that rises above the land around it

island a landform with water all around it

lake a body of water with land on all sides

mountain highest kind of land

ocean a body of salt water that covers a large area

peninsula a landform that is surrounded on only three sides by water

plain flat land

river a large stream of water that flows across the land

valley low land between hills or mountains

Rules and Laws

Start with the Standards

1.1 Students describe the rights and individual responsibilities of citizenship.

The Big Idea

Citizenship

Rules and laws guide people to live safely and be responsible citizens.

What to Know

✔ Why should we follow rules?

✔ How do laws help communities?

✔ How do community leaders help people?

✔ How can you show respect for others?

Show What You Know

★ Unit I Test

✎ Writing: A List

🖌 Unit Project: A Campaign Rally

Unit 1 Rules and Laws

Talk About

Citizenship

" Your country needs you. "

"Everyone should vote."

"Respect people's rights."

VOTE

Vocabulary

community A group of people who live and work together. It is also the place where they live. (page 18)

citizen A person who lives in and belongs to a community. (page 18)

rule An instruction that tells people how to act. (page 12)

law A rule that people in a community must follow. (page 19)

vote A choice that gets counted. (page 26)

GO ONLINE

INTERNET RESOURCES
Go to **www.harcourtschool.com/hss** to view Internet resources for this unit.

Reading Social Studies

Focus Skill: Cause and Effect

As you read, think about why the things you are reading about happen.

● A cause is what makes something happen.

● What happens is the effect.

Practice the Skill

Read the paragraphs.

Cause
Effect
Anna has work to do at home. She puts her things away so they do not get lost. She helps her mom set the table for dinner. She helps her dad fold the clothes. Anna's little brother, Jon, can't read yet, so she tells him stories.

When Anna has finished her work, she can have fun. No one in Anna's family has too much to do because everyone helps with the work.

4

Apply What You Learned

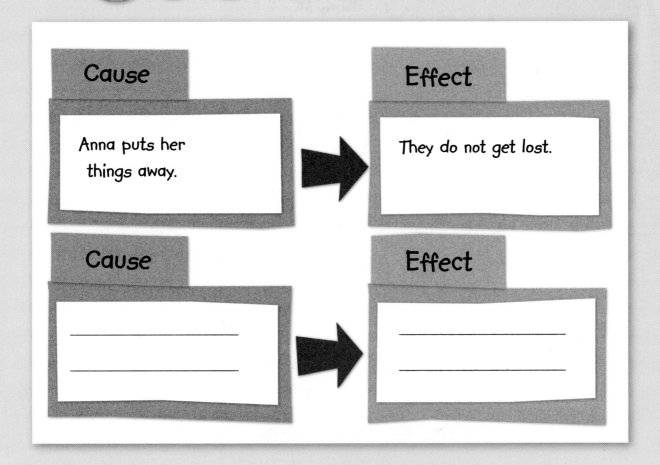

Cause		Effect
Anna puts her things away.	→	They do not get lost.
Cause		Effect
_____ _____	→	_____ _____

The chart shows one cause and effect from the story. What is another cause and effect from the story? Copy the chart and fill it in.

Apply as You Read

As you read, think about ways the things you do affect others.

5

Study Skills

Preview and Question

New ideas are easier to understand when you write what you have learned. A K-W-L chart helps you write down important facts before and after you read.

Practice the Skill

The K-W-L chart on the next page shows what Angel knows about voting. Copy the chart.

- What do you already know about voting? Write it under What I Know.

- What do you want to know about voting? Write it under What I Want to Know.

K-W-L Chart

What I Know	What I Want to Know	What I Learned
People vote to make choices.	Where do people vote?	

Read the paragraph. Write the new facts you learn under What I Learned.

People vote at schools, churches, and other places near their homes. People vote by marking ballots to show their choices. A person can vote only once. All votes are counted to see which choice wins.

Apply as You Read

Make a K-W-L chart to show what you know and want to know about rules and laws. As you read, add facts to the chart to show what you have learned.

Friendship's Rule

by M. Lucille Ford

illustrated by Stacy Peterson

Our teacher says there is a rule
We should remember while at school,

At home, at play, whate'er we do,
And that's the rule of friendship true.

If you would have friends, you must do
To them the kindly things that you

Would like to have them do and say
To you while at your work and play.

And that's the rule of friendship true;
It works in all we say and do.

It pays to be a friend polite,
For friendship's rule is always right.

Response Corner

1. What is friendship's rule?

2. **Make It Relevant** Draw a picture of you and a friend following friendship's rule.

School Rules

What to Know
Why should we follow rules?

✔ Rules help us get along and be fair.

✔ We have a responsibility to follow rules.

Vocabulary
teacher
rule
responsibility
principal
fair

Focus Skill Cause and Effect

California Standards
HSS 1.1, 1.1.2

Our **teacher** leads the class. She helps us make the class rules. A **rule** tells people how to act. We follow rules when we work and when we play.

At school, rules help us learn and get along. This is why we have a responsibility to follow rules. A **responsibility** is something you should do.

Be kind.

Follow directions.

Work quietly.

Take turns.

Our **principal** leads the whole school. He tells us that different parts of the school have different rules. We walk quietly in the hall. When we play outside, we do not have to be quiet.

Our principal also tells us that rules help us be fair. Being **fair** means that we act in a way that is right and honest.

Summary Rules help us get along and be fair. We have a responsibility to follow rules.

Review

1. 💡 Why should we follow rules?

2. **Vocabulary** What does it mean to be **fair**?

3. ✏️ **Write** Write a sentence that tells one of your classroom rules.

4. ⭐ (Focus Skill) **Cause and Effect** What may happen if a rule is broken?

15

Solve a Problem

❱ Why It Matters

A **problem** is something that is hard to solve, or fix. A **solution** is one answer to a problem. Working together can make solving a problem easier.

❱ What You Need to Know

1 Make sure each person knows the problem.

2 List different solutions that may solve the problem. Talk about what is good or bad about each solution.

3 Work together to choose the solution that makes the most people happy. Then see how well it works.

Take turns.

❯ Practice the Skill

Before Think of something you have to use with others.

During Make a list of ways to use it fairly. Choose the best solution and try it.

After Talk about how well the solution worked.

❯ Apply What You Learned

Make It Relevant Work as a group to solve another problem in your classroom. List some solutions, and choose one that makes the most people happy.

Community Rules

What to Know
How do laws help communities?

✔ Laws tell people in a community how to act.

✔ Laws help make communities safe.

Vocabulary
community
citizen
law

 **Cause and Effect**

 California Standards
HSS 1.1, 1.1.2

This is my community. A **community** is a place where people live and work together. A person who lives in and belongs to a community is a **citizen**.

Communities have rules called laws. A **law** is a rule that people in a community must follow. Communities can have many kinds of laws.

Huntington Beach, California

Laws are important for citizens in a community. They tell people how to live together safely. Police officers make sure that people follow the laws.

⚡*Fast Fact*

In Los Angeles County, California, it is against the law to roller-skate at a library. Is this a good law? Why or why not?

Sometimes people do not follow laws. Breaking laws causes problems. People who cross the street at the wrong place may get hurt.

Summary Laws help people live together safely in a community.

Review

1. How do laws help communities?

2. **Vocabulary** What is a **citizen**?

3. **Activity** Draw a picture that shows you and your family following a law in your community.

4. **Cause and Effect** What can happen if you do not follow a law?

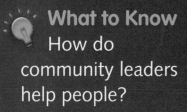

Lesson 3

Our Leaders

What to Know

How do community leaders help people?

✓ Leaders help groups follow rules and solve problems.

✓ People can choose their leaders.

Vocabulary
leader
group
mayor
city
government

Focus Skill

Cause and Effect

California Standards
HSS 1.1, 1.1.1

Yim Kwan came to the opening of our community's new school. He is a community leader. A **leader** is a person who is in charge of a group. A **group** is a number of people working together.

22

Leaders help groups make and follow rules. They also help groups solve problems.

Yim Kwan is our mayor. A **mayor** is the leader of a city. A **city** is a large community.

Mayor Kwan

Mayor Kwan helps open our new school.

23

People in a community choose the leaders they want for their government. A **government** is a group of people who lead a community. Mayor Kwan leads the city government.

Geography

Sacramento

The city of Sacramento is the capital of the state of California. The capital is the city in which the state government meets. The governor, who is the leader of the state government, works in the capital.

There are many kinds of leaders in our community. My mom is a baseball coach, so she is a leader. Teachers, club leaders, and ministers are also leaders.

Summary Leaders help people follow rules and solve problems in the community.

Review

1. 💡 How do community leaders help people?

2. **Vocabulary** What does a **mayor** do?

3. ✏️ **Activity** Draw a picture that shows a leader helping people in your community.

4. ⭐ **Cause and Effect** Think about a time when a leader helped you solve a problem. What did he or she do?

Make a Choice by Voting

❯ Why It Matters

When you **vote**, you make a choice that gets counted. In schools and in communities, people vote for rules and leaders. Sometimes everyone votes on rules. Other times people vote for leaders to make the rules for them.

Americans vote for many government leaders, such as the President. The **President** is the leader of our country. Americans also vote to make choices about laws.

❯ What You Need to Know

You can use a ballot to vote. A **ballot** is a paper that shows all the choices. You mark your choice on it. The choice that gets the most votes wins.

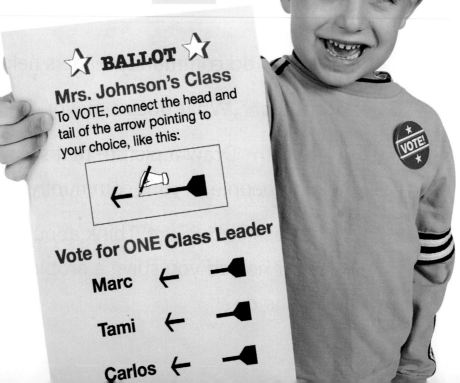

☆ **BALLOT** ☆
Mrs. Johnson's Class
To VOTE, connect the head and tail of the arrow pointing to your choice, like this:

Vote for ONE Class Leader

Marc ←   ◄

Tami ←   ◄

Carlos ←   ◄

Practice the Skill

1 Mrs. Johnson's class used ballots to vote for a class leader. The choices were Marc, Tami, and Carlos.

2 Look at the chart. Count all the votes to see who will be the class leader.

Apply What You Learned

Make It Relevant List some games your class would like to play. Make ballots, and have each person vote. Count the votes and show them on a chart. Which game got the most votes?

Trustworthiness

Respect
Responsibility
Fairness
Caring
Patriotism

Why Character Counts

❓ **Why do you think people trusted George Washington?**

George Washington was the first President of the United States.

George Washington

George Washington thought that people should work hard and be honest. He started working when he was 17 years old. He helped people make maps of their land. He was so honest and fair that many people wanted him to work for them. Later, Washington joined the army and became a trusted leader.

As a young man, Washington owned and worked with land.

Washington was a kind and fair leader. He rewarded people for their hard work.

Washington led Americans in a fight to be free and to rule their own country. When the United States began, Americans chose him to be their first President. Thomas Jefferson once wrote about him, "He was . . . a wise, a good, and a great man."*

*Thomas Jefferson, from a letter to Dr. Walter Jones, January 2, 1814

Interactive Multimedia Biographies
Visit MULTIMEDIA BIOGRAPHIES
at **www.harcourtschool.com/hss**

Bio Brief

1732   1799

Important Dates

1759 Marries Martha Dandridge

1775 Becomes a leader in the army

1787 Helps write the United States Constitution

1789 Becomes the first President of the United States

The Golden Rule

What to Know
How can you show respect for others?

✔ We can respect people's rights.

✔ We can be responsible citizens.

Vocabulary
respect
right

Cause and Effect

California Standards
HSS 1.1, 1.1.2

To show **respect** is to treat someone or something well. I show respect for my teacher by listening to him and following rules.

The Golden Rule says to treat others the way you want to be treated. I can use the Golden Rule to remember to respect others.

Cultural Heritage

Confucius

A wise man in China taught the Golden Rule more than 2,500 years ago. His name was Confucius. Confucius believed that people should always respect others. He also said, "Respect yourself and others will respect you." *

*Confucius, from The Confucian Analects, ca. 500 B.C.

Americans have rights. A **right** is something people are free to do. We can show respect for the rights of others.

Free to worship

Free to speak

We can also show respect for others by being responsible in the way we act. When we follow rules and laws, we show respect for other people's rights.

Summary We can show respect for others by being responsible.

Review

1. How can you show respect for others?

2. **Vocabulary** What is one **right** that you have?

3. **Activity** Act out some ways people follow the Golden Rule.

4. **Focus Skill** **Cause and Effect** What may happen if you do not respect the rights of others?

Work and Play Together

▶ Why It Matters

It is important to show respect for others when we do things together.

▶ What You Need to Know

1 We **share** when we use something with others.

2 We show good **sportsmanship** when we play fairly.

3 When we work or play together, we show respect by sharing and by playing fairly. When we do not agree, we listen to each person's ideas. Then we work together to find a solution.

❱ Practice the Skill

Before   Think of something your class could do as a group. You might choose to make a rule, plan a party, or paint a mural.

During   Give everyone a chance to share ideas.

After   Talk about how well the people in your group worked together.

❱ Apply What You Learned

Make It Relevant   Work with a group to make up a game. Use what you have learned about working and playing together.

Police Officers and You

Police officers help us follow rules and laws. They teach us ways we can live safely and responsibly in our community. Some police officers also work in schools. These officers are called school resource officers.

School resource officers help children treat each other fairly. Children know their school's officers by name. They know that when they need help, the officers will be there.

Police officers also help children have fun. A group called the Police Activities League, or PAL, gives children a safe place to play sports and have fun.

School resource officer

Police officers help us have fun, too.

You can learn more about laws and rules from police officers. That is how Heather Fong got the idea to become a police officer.

"A police officer came to our high school and talked about law enforcement careers," says Fong. Now she is the chief of police in San Francisco.

San Francisco Police Chief Heather Fong

Did You Know?

Did you know that the Police Activities League (PAL) gives children great ways to meet and play?

★ PAL welcomes children from ages 6 to 17.
★ PAL teaches good sportsmanship in games, such as soccer and baseball.
★ Your town or city may have a PAL.

Think About It!

Make It Relevant How do police officers help people in your community?

The Lion and the Mouse

an Aesop fable
illustrated by David Diaz

Lion   Mouse   First Hunter   Second Hunter   Third Hunter

Setting: A sleeping lion's den
The mouse enters.

Mouse: I see a small piece of food by that big lion. He is fast asleep. I will sneak by him and grab the food before he wakes up.

The mouse creeps in to pick up the food. Suddenly, the lion wakes up and slaps his paw down on the mouse's tail.

Lion: Now I've got you, and I am very hungry. I will eat you in one gulp!

Mouse: No! Please let me go!

Lion: Why should I? You will be very tasty.

Mouse: A mouse is not good to eat. I am only skin and bones.

Lion: It is true that you are very tiny.

Mouse: Yes, and if you let me go, I will do something good for you one day.

Lion: Ha! How could a little mouse ever help a big lion?

Mouse: Oh, you will see if you let me go.

Lion: Well, all right. Now leave before I change my mind and eat you!

Mouse: Thank you, kind lion!

The mouse runs away, and the lion goes back to sleep. Three hunters enter, holding a net.

First Hunter: There! The lion is fast asleep. We can catch him.

Second Hunter: What if he wakes up?

Third Hunter: We will move very quietly.

The hunters move slowly toward the lion.

First Hunter: Let's try it!

Second Hunter : Yes, get the net ready!

Third Hunter: Let's go!

The hunters quickly throw the net over the lion. The lion wakes up and tries to get out of the net.

Lion: Help! Help me!

First Hunter: Silly lion, you can't get out. Our net is too strong for you!

Second Hunter : This lion is too big for the three of us to carry. Let's go back to town to get help.

The hunters leave.

Lion: Help! Someone please help me!

The mouse enters.

Mouse: Lion, I heard you yelling. What happened?

Lion: Hunters have trapped me. I can't get loose!

Mouse: I can help you. I will chew through the net with my sharp teeth.

The mouse chews on the net, and finally the lion is free.

Lion: Thank you so much, little mouse! You are a good friend.

Mouse: Even a little mouse can be a big help.

The End

Response Corner

❶ How does the mouse show that he is responsible?

❷ **Make It Relevant** Write a sentence about a time when someone helped you.

The Capitol

Get Ready

The California state government works in Sacramento in the capitol building. People visit the capitol to learn about California. They enjoy its museum, gardens, and statues.

Locate It
California

Sacramento

What to See

The California state seal

42

Inside the capitol, you can see where the government meets to talk about laws. You can also see this statue of Columbus and Queen Isabella of Spain.

The Mexican and Spanish seal

The capitol has a beautiful park with a rose garden.

This statue honors firefighters who work to keep California citizens safe.

A Virtual Tour

GO
ONLINE   Visit VIRTUAL TOURS at
www.harcourtschool.com/hss

Review

Citizenship Rules and laws guide people to live safely and be responsible citizens.

Focus Skill Cause and Effect

Copy and fill in the chart to show what you have learned about rules and responsibility.

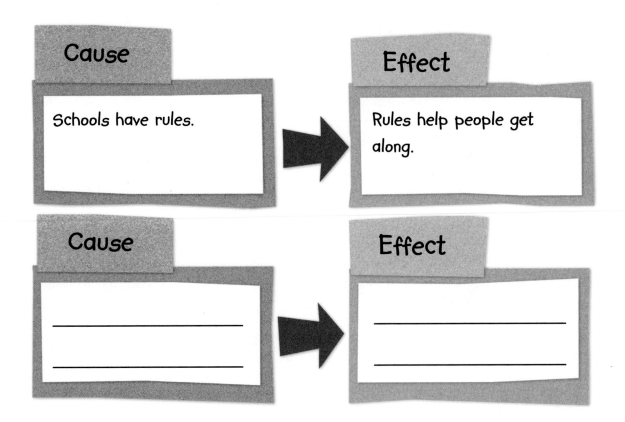

Cause

Schools have rules.

Effect

Rules help people get along.

Cause

_____
_____

Effect

_____
_____

Use Vocabulary

Write the word that goes with each meaning.

1 a person who lives in and belongs to a community

2 a rule that people in a community must follow

3 a choice that gets counted

4 an instruction that tells people how to act

5 a place where people live and work together

rule
(p. 12)
community
(p. 18)
citizen
(p. 18)
law
(p. 19)
vote
(p. 26)

Recall Facts

6 Why do we have a responsibility to follow rules?

7 What does it mean to be fair?

8 Who chooses leaders in a community?

9 Which person leads the city government?

    A police officer   **C** mayor

    B citizen   **D** teacher

10 Which action does NOT follow the Golden Rule?

    A sharing   **C** taking turns

    B breaking laws   **D** listening to others

Think Critically

11. **ANALYSIS SKILL** What would happen if there were no laws in your community?

12. **Make It Relevant** What new rule would you make for your classroom? What makes this a good rule?

Apply Critical Thinking Skills

13. What is the problem?

14. How many solutions are listed?

15. Which solution do you think is the best?

16. Why do you like that solution best?

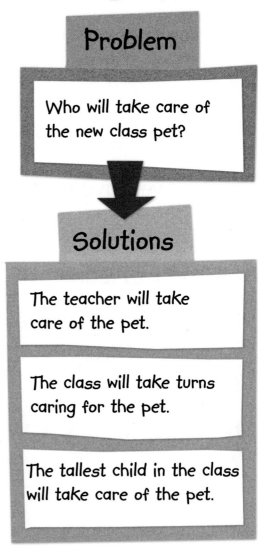

Problem

Who will take care of the new class pet?

Solutions

The teacher will take care of the pet.

The class will take turns caring for the pet.

The tallest child in the class will take care of the pet.

Apply Participation Skills

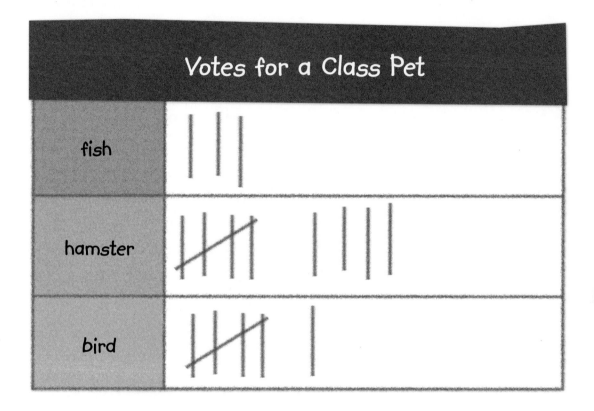

Votes for a Class Pet

fish				
hamster	||||| ||||
bird	|||||	

17 How did the children in this class choose a pet?

18 Which pet did the class choose?

19 How many children voted for the bird?

20 Which pet got the fewest votes?

Unit 1 Activities

Read More

Garrett Morgan
by Susan Ring

School and Community Rules
by Sheila Sweeny

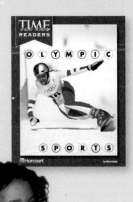

Olympic Sports
by Ellen Catala

Show What You Know

Unit Writing Activity

Think about School Rules
Imagine that a new child comes to your class. How would you help this person learn the rules?

Write a List Write a list of school rules. Draw pictures of your classmates following each rule.

Unit Project

Campaign Rally Plan a campaign rally.

- Choose two people to run for Class Safety Monitor.
- Make posters and signs.
- Tell about safety rules at the rally.

GO ONLINE Visit ACTIVITIES at www.harcourtschool.com/hss

48

Where People Live

 Start with the Standards

1.2 Students compare and contrast the absolute and relative locations of places and people and describe the physical and/or human characteristics of places.

The Big Idea

Places

People live in many different locations. Where people are affects the way they live.

What to Know

✓ How can a map help you find places?

✓ What can pictures, maps, and models show you?

✓ How do location, land, and resources affect the way people live?

✓ How does weather affect people?

Show What You Know

★ Unit 2 Test

✎ Writing: A Letter

 Unit Project: A "Places We Live" Mural

Where People Live

Talk About

Places

" California is a big state with many kinds of places and people. "

THE UNITED STATES OF AMERICA

"There are large cities along the Pacific Ocean."

"Many things grow in California."

49

Vocabulary

state A part of a country.

(page 59)

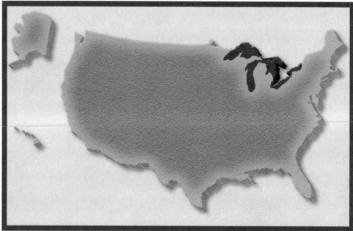

country An area of land with its own people and laws. (page 60)

globe A model of Earth. (page 62)

School

Fire Station

Market

Hospital

House

continent A large area of land. (page 62)

symbol A picture or an object that stands for something. (page 68)

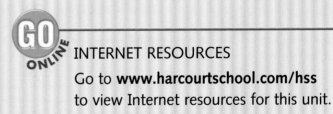

GO ONLINE INTERNET RESOURCES
Go to **www.harcourtschool.com/hss** to view Internet resources for this unit.

Reading Social Studies

Categorize and Classify

As you read, categorize and classify information.

- To categorize, you put things into groups to show how they are the same.

- To classify, you decide if something fits into a group.

Practice the Skill

Read the paragraphs.

Classify
Categorize

California has many places to visit. People go to San Diego, Los Angeles, and other cities. Families visit theme parks such as SeaWorld and Disneyland.

Other people come to California to see national parks. They visit Yosemite National Park and Redwood National Park. They also go to see deserts such as the Mojave Desert and Death Valley.

Yosemite National Park

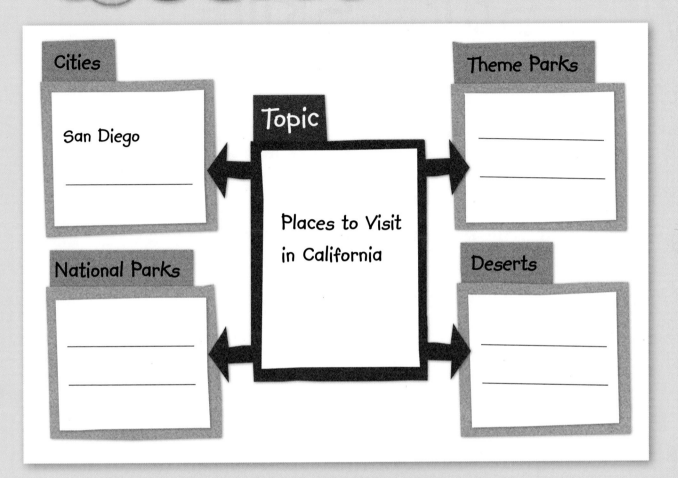

Cities

San Diego

_____

Topic

Places to Visit
in California

Theme Parks

_____

_____

National Parks

_____

_____

Deserts

_____

_____

Copy this chart. Then use it to categorize and classify the places in California that you just read about. Put each place into a group.

Apply as You Read

As you read, look for ways to categorize and classify other places in California.

Study Skills

Build Vocabulary

As you read, you will come to many new words. You can write these words in a web to help you learn them.

Practice the Skill

The word web on the next page shows how Harry grouped words about places. Copy the web.

- What word is in the middle circle?

- Why is <u>California</u> in one of the other circles?

California   places   ocean

Read the paragraph. Which words are kinds of places? Add these words to your word web.

California is a great place to visit. You can swim and find shells at the ocean. You can ride a bike through the hills and valleys. You can also hike in the forests. There are many things to do for fun in California.

Apply as You Read

Make a web for the word **map**. As you read this unit, add words to your web that tell about maps.

Making Maps

by Elaine V. Emans
illustrated by Rob Dunlavey

I love to make maps!
I think it's great fun—
Making the boundaries,
And then, one by one,
Putting in railroads,
And each river bend,
And the tiny towns
Where little roads end.

I draw in mountains,
And often a lake,
And I've even had
Long bridges to make!
I like to do highways,
And when they are drawn
I dream that they take me
Where I've never gone.

Response Corner

1 What kinds of things can you find on a map?

2 **Make It Relevant** Draw a map of a place that you make up.

57

What to Know

How can a map help you find places?

✔ Maps show locations.

✔ Maps show land and water.

Vocabulary
location
map
state
country
border

Focus Skill Categorize and Classify

California Standards
HSS 1.2, 1.2.1

Finding Where You Are

A **location** is the place where something is. A **map** is a picture that shows locations. This map shows the locations of places in a community.

ANALYSIS SKILL What places can you find on this map?

Hospital

Oak Drive

Post Office

School

My House

Main Street

Market

Central Avenue

Park

Park Street

Maple Lane

Maps can show many kinds of places. One map may show streets in a city. Another may show cities in a **state**. California is a state. San Jose is a city.

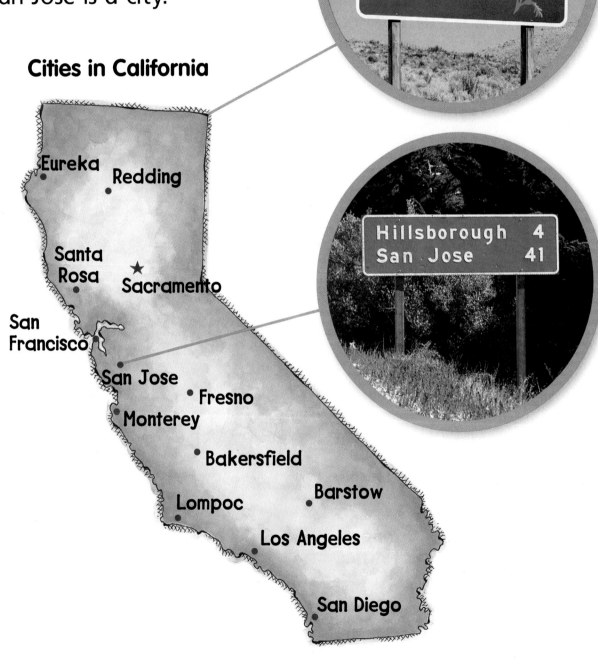

Cities in California

Eureka

Redding

Santa Rosa

★ Sacramento

San Francisco

San Jose

Monterey

Fresno

Bakersfield

Barstow

Lompoc

Los Angeles

San Diego

Welcome to California

Hillsborough 4
San Jose 41

 ANALYSIS SKILL Where is San Jose on this map?

Some maps show states and countries. A **country** is an area of land with its own people and laws. The United States of America is our country. It has 50 states.

Lines on a map show borders. A **border** is where a state or country ends.

United States

ALASKA

CANADA

WASHINGTON
OREGON
IDAHO
MONTANA
NORTH DAKOTA
SOUTH DAKOTA
WYOMING
MINNESOTA
WISCONSIN
MICHIGAN
NEW HAMPSHIRE
VERMONT
MAINE
NEW YORK
MASSACHUSETTS
RHODE ISLAND
NEVADA
UTAH
COLORADO
NEBRASKA
IOWA
ILLINOIS
INDIANA
OHIO
PENNSYLVANIA
CONNECTICUT
NEW JERSEY
DELAWARE
MARYLAND
Washington, D.C.
CALIFORNIA
KANSAS
MISSOURI
KENTUCKY
WEST VIRGINIA
VIRGINIA
NORTH CAROLINA
ARIZONA
NEW MEXICO
OKLAHOMA
ARKANSAS
TENNESSEE
SOUTH CAROLINA
GEORGIA
PACIFIC OCEAN
TEXAS
MISSISSIPPI
ALABAMA
LOUISIANA
FLORIDA
ATLANTIC OCEAN
HAWAII
MEXICO
Gulf of Mexico

ANALYSIS SKILL Find the United States of America and California on this map.

Most maps use colors to show land and water. Green or brown shows land. Blue shows water. Rivers are blue lines on a map. Sometimes they are the borders of states.

Summary Maps show the locations of places such as streets, cities, states, countries, rivers, and oceans.

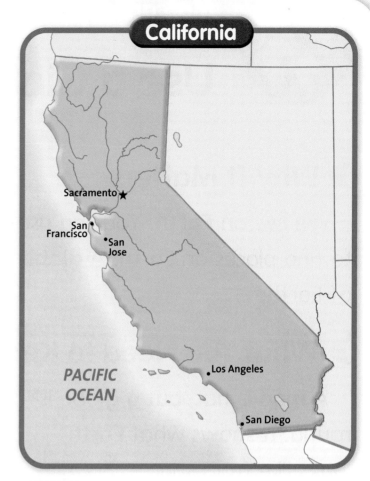

California

Sacramento ★

San Francisco

San Jose

PACIFIC OCEAN

Los Angeles

San Diego

ANALYSIS SKILL What ocean borders California?

Review

❶ How can a map help you find places?

❷ **Vocabulary** What is a **country**?

❸ **Write** Look at a map. Write sentences that tell where you live.

❹ **Categorize and Classify** What is brown or green on a map? What is blue?

Use a Globe

❱ Why It Matters

We live on **Earth**. You can use a globe to find places on Earth. A **globe** is a model of Earth.

❱ What You Need to Know

A map is flat, but a globe is round. It shows what Earth looks like from space.

Like a map, a globe shows locations of places. Each large area of land is a **continent**. Each large body of water is an **ocean**.

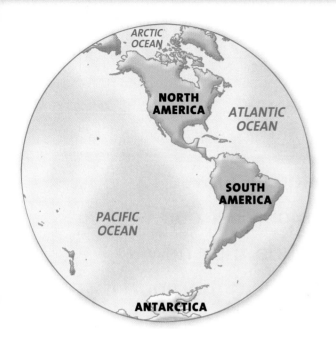

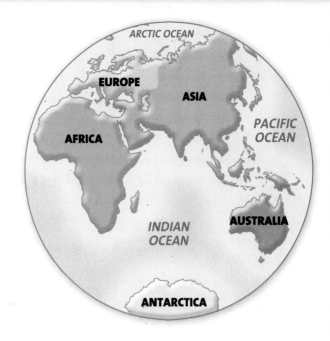

Practice the Skill

1 Look at the drawings of a globe. Find and name the continent on which you live.

2 Use your finger to follow the border around South America.

3 Which ocean is between Australia and Africa?

Apply What You Learned

ANALYSIS SKILL Look at a globe. Find and name the seven continents and the four oceans.

 Practice your map and globe skills with the **GeoSkills CD-ROM**.

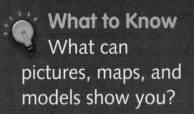
 What to Know
What can pictures, maps, and models show you?

✓ Pictures, maps, and models all show places.

✓ Pictures, maps, and models can show the same place in different ways.

Vocabulary
neighborhood

 **Categorize and Classify**

California Standards
HSS 1.2, 1.2.2

Neighborhood Map

When Kim's family moved to a new city, Kim and her dad took a walk around their new neighborhood. A **neighborhood** is a part of a town or city.

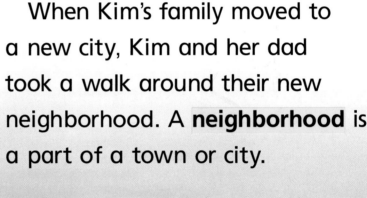

Kim's dad showed her a map of the neighborhood. They found the location of Kim's new school. Kim took pictures of places as they walked.

Later, Kim and her dad looked at the pictures. The pictures showed some of the places on the map. The places in the pictures and the places on the map looked different.

Kim used her pictures and the map to make a model of places in her neighborhood. Pictures and maps are flat, but you can look at a model from all sides. When Kim looks down at the top of her model, it is like looking at a map.

Summary You can learn about a place by looking at a picture, a map, or a model. Each shows the same place in a different way.

Review

1. What can pictures, maps, and models show you?

2. **Vocabulary** What can you find in a **neighborhood**?

3. **Activity** Make a model like Kim's to show your neighborhood.

4. **Categorize and Classify** How are maps like globes and pictures?

Read a Map

❯ Why It Matters

You can use symbols to help you read a map. A **symbol** is a picture or an object that stands for something.

❯ What You Need to Know

Maps use symbols to show places. A **map legend** shows you what each symbol on the map stands for.

❯ Practice the Skill

❶ What places do you see on the map?

❷ What symbol shows the fire station?

❸ Where would you go in this neighborhood to buy food?

Map Legend

School

Fire Station

Market

Hospital

House

Apartment Building

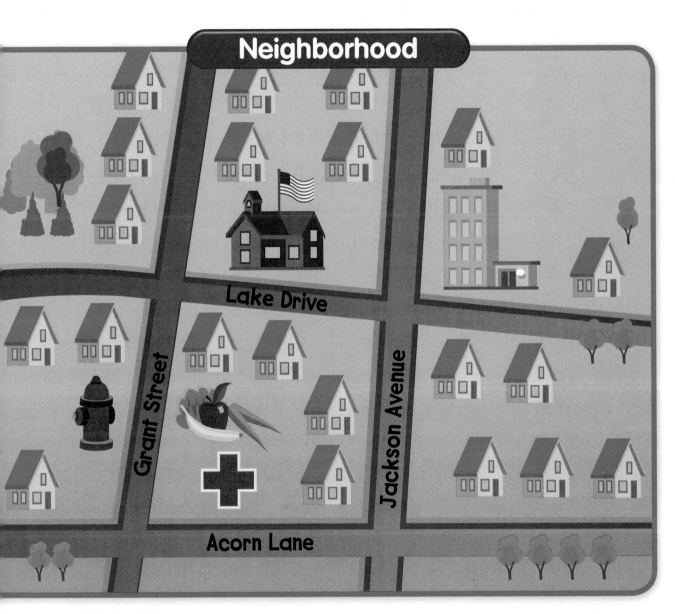

Neighborhood

Lake Drive

Grant Street

Jackson Avenue

Acorn Lane

🌙 Apply What You Learned

ANALYSIS SKILL **Make It Relevant** Make a map of your school. Use symbols and a map legend to show places.

 Practice your map and globe skills with the **GeoSkills CD-ROM.**

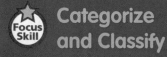

The Land Around You

Different parts of California have different kinds of land. People can live near mountains or forests, on hills, or in valleys or deserts. They can also live by lakes, rivers, or the ocean.

What to Know
How do location, land, and resources affect the way people live?

✔ People live in different places in California.

✔ Where people live affects how they live.

Vocabulary
resource
farm
shelter
transportation

 **Categorize and Classify**

California Standards
HSS 1.2, 1.2.4

hills

mountain

70

Each kind of land has resources. A **resource** is anything that people can use. Soil, trees, and water are some of Earth's resources.

A place's location, land, and resources affect what people eat, where they live, and how they move around.

People build dams to store water.

forest

desert

ocean

People use resources to grow food on farms. A **farm** is a place for growing plants and raising animals. Many kinds of food that you eat come from farms all over the country.

People who live near water often fish for food. People in other places grow trees to get food. Fruits and nuts grow on trees.

Imperial Valley, California

Ways We Use Land and Water

sheep

almonds

fish

People need shelter. A **shelter** is a home. People in different places build different kinds of shelters.

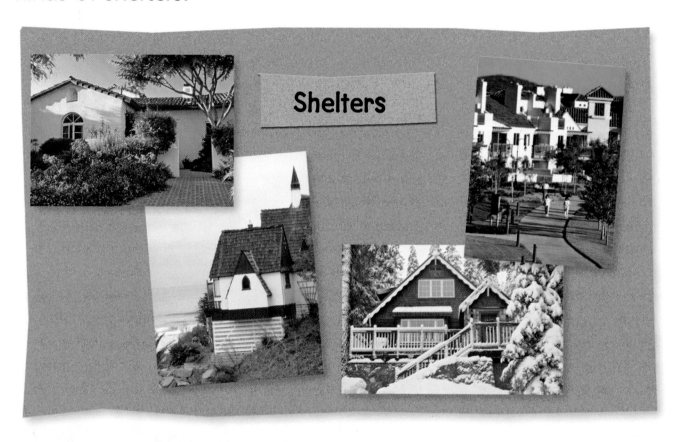

Shelters

Adobe Houses

Casa del Oro

Long ago, Spanish settlers came to California. They learned from the people who lived there how to make houses out of sun-baked mud, called adobe. You can still see old adobe houses in Monterey County, California.

People also need transportation. **Transportation** is any way of moving people and things from place to place. Transportation can be by land, water, or air.

Transportation

Summary California has many kinds of places and resources. Where people live affects their food, shelter, and transportation.

Review

1. 💡 How do location, land, and resources affect the way people live?

2. **Vocabulary** What is a **resource**?

3. ✏️ **Activity** Make a book about places in California. Show the place where you live.

4. ⭐ **Categorize and Classify** Make a chart showing kinds of transportation that go by land, by water, and by air.

Find Directions on a Map

❯ Why It Matters

Directions point the way to places. They help you find locations.

❯ What You Need to Know

The four main directions are called **cardinal directions**. They are north, south, east, and west. If you face north, west is on your left. East is on your right. South is behind you.

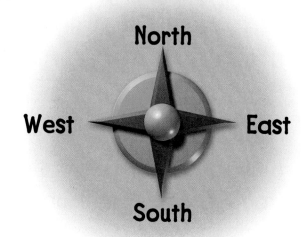

❯ Practice the Skill

❶ What is east of the parking lot?

❷ What is north of the school buildings?

❸ Find the school garden. Now move your finger to the parking lot. In which direction did you move?

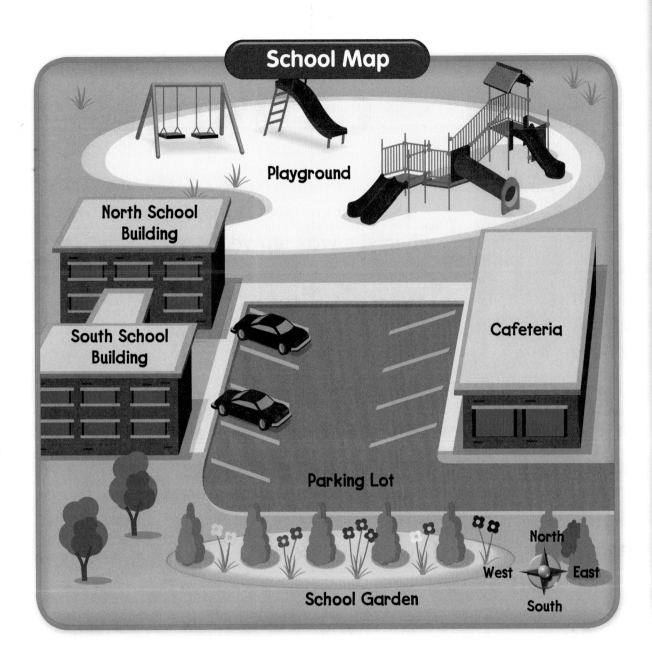

School Map

Playground

North School Building

South School Building

Cafeteria

Parking Lot

North
West • East
South

School Garden

◗ Apply What You Learned

 ANALYSIS SKILL **Make It Relevant** Make a map of your classroom. Show directions.

Practice your map and globe skills with the **GeoSkills CD-ROM.**

Trustworthiness
Respect
Responsibility
Fairness
Caring
Patriotism

Why Character Counts

❖ **How did Rachel Carson show that she cared about nature?**

Rachel Carson was a writer and scientist who taught people to keep nature safe.

Rachel Carson

Rachel Carson wrote her first story when she was ten years old. Even then, she knew she wanted to be a writer. She also cared about nature. She played in the woods around her home and drew pictures of animals. "There was no time when I wasn't interested in . . . the whole world of nature,"* Rachel Carson later said.

*Rachel Carson, from a public statement, 1954

Rachel Carson grew up in the country and loved to be outdoors.

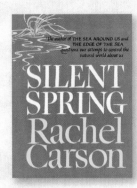

Rachel Carson once wrote, "The beauty of the living world that I was trying to save has always been . . . in my mind. . ."*

*Rachel Carson, from a letter to a friend, 1962

Bio Brief

1907   1964

Important Dates

1918 Writes her first story, at the age of ten

1932 Graduates from the University of Maryland

1962 Writes her most famous book, Silent Spring

1980 Wins the Presidential Medal of Freedom after her death

Rachel Carson wrote about birds, plants, and the ocean. She believed that everyone has a responsibility to care for Earth. In 1962, she wrote a book called Silent Spring. In it, she told people about the dangers of pesticides, or poisons used to kill insects. The pesticides were also killing birds and plants. Because of Rachel Carson's book, better laws were made to keep nature safe.

GO ONLINE Interactive Multimedia Biographies Visit MULTIMEDIA BIOGRAPHIES at **www.harcourtschool.com/hss**

What's the Weather?

California has many kinds of weather. **Weather** is the way the air feels outside.

What to Know
How does weather affect people?

✔ There are four seasons.

✔ People in California enjoy many kinds of recreation.

Vocabulary
weather
season
recreation

 **Focus Skill** Categorize and Classify

California Standards
HSS 1.2, 1.2.4

Weather changes with the seasons. A **season** is a time of year. The four seasons are spring, summer, fall, and winter.

A season's weather is different in different places. In California, not all places have snow in the winter.

Spring

Summer

Fall

Winter

People check the weather before they decide what to wear. They choose clothes that will keep them warm, dry, or cool.

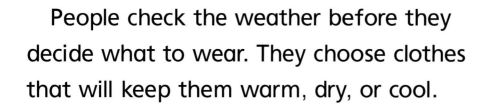

⚡Fast Fact

The hottest place in the United States is a desert in California called Death Valley. One time, it was 134 degrees in Death Valley!

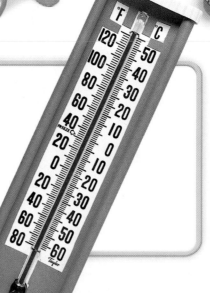

People also choose their recreation to go with the weather. **Recreation** is what people do for fun. Playing sports or games and enjoying the outdoors are kinds of recreation.

Summary California has many kinds of weather. The weather affects how we dress and how we play.

Review

① How does weather affect people?

② **Vocabulary** What are the four **seasons**?

③ **Activity** Be a weather reporter. Tell people what clothes to wear for each kind of weather you report.

④ **Categorize and Classify** Make a chart that shows ways to have fun in summer and in winter.

Points of View

The Sidewalk Reporter asks:

"What is special about the place where you live?"

Eddie

"I can swim at the beach in summer and ski in the mountains in winter."

Mrs. Johnson

"People come from all over to see our beautiful butterflies."

View from the Past

James Marshall: The Gold Rush

Long ago, gold made California a special place to live. In 1848, James Marshall found gold by the American River. This news spread quickly, and the California gold rush began.

Erin

"We have a good bus system. It makes it easy to get around the community."

Ms. Patel

"We have hundreds of places to eat that have foods of every kind."

Mr. Ruiz

"I catch fish in the many lakes and rivers near our community."

ANALYSIS SKILL It's Your Turn

- Does your community have any of these special things? If so, which ones?
- What makes your community special?

Those Building Men

by Angela Johnson
illustrated by Barry Moser

Past the ocean waves,
and into the woods,
past the plains
and over the mountains,
worked those shadowy
building men—

Our fathers. . . .
Poor and sometimes
from far away,
but looking ahead. . . .
And building it all.

The prairies rolled into
mountains' majesty.

86

But they hammered and laid
hard steel along it.
Cook camps, hard work,
and all of them far from home. . . .
Those railroad workers,
those blue-sky working men.

You can hear the echoes
of the ones who were there
to connect it all.
And when the roads came through
with our fathers saying,
"Ain't that something,"
as the trees and mountains
came down.

The fathers' skin burnt in the sun
at the backbreaking work,
but they'd look back and say,
"Ain't that something."
"Yeah, ain't that something."

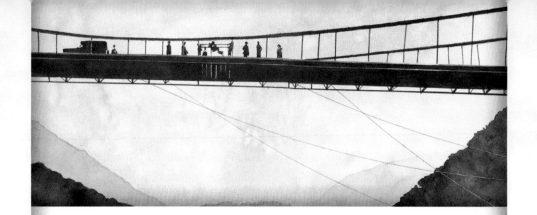

As buildings tower above us,
they tell the tales
of the cities. . . .

They whisper down past it all and say,
"They built us; your fathers.
Walls of steel,
towers tall,
their hands so strong.

"Fearless air climbers,
those fearless air-climbing men.

"And all those sky walkers,
surefooted sky walkers,
native sky walkers.

"Bridging, bridges.

"Those steel cables
singing in the wind.
Over it all,
yes, over it all."

Now we look on it all
and remember our fathers.
Those building men.
Those strong,
but now shadowy,
building men.

Response Corner

1 What kinds of places does this poem talk about?

2 **Make It Relevant** This poem talks about many things that were built. What do builders build in your community?

Field Trip

Point Reyes
National Seashore

Get Ready

Point Reyes National Seashore is a good place to enjoy California's different kinds of land. The rocky coasts, beaches, hills, and forests have many plants and animals. You can even see seals and whales!

Locate It
California

Point Reyes

What to See

This lighthouse was built many years ago. It let ships know they were near land in foggy weather.

Tule elks are found only in California.

Point Reyes National Park has more than 140 miles of hiking trails.

Many ocean animals, such as these sea stars, live at Point Reyes.

Sea lions and seals rest along the seashore.

A Virtual Tour

GO ONLINE

Visit VIRTUAL TOURS at
www.harcourtschool.com/hss

Review

💡 **Places** People live in many different locations. Where people live affects the way they live.

(Focus Skill) Categorize and Classify

Copy and fill in the chart to categorize and classify clothing for different kinds of weather.

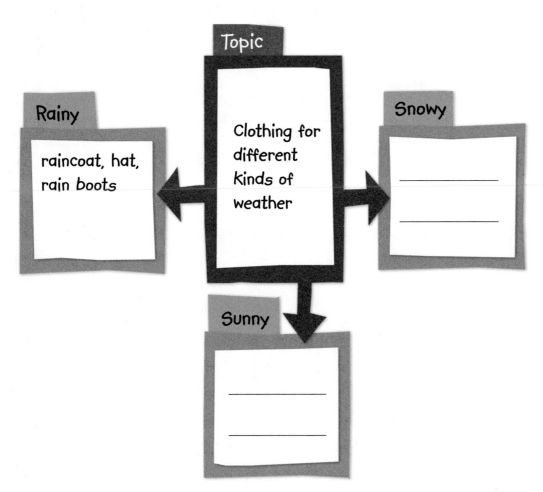

Topic

Clothing for different Kinds of weather

Rainy

raincoat, hat, rain boots

Snowy

_____

_____

Sunny

_____

_____

Use Vocabulary

Write the word that goes with each picture.

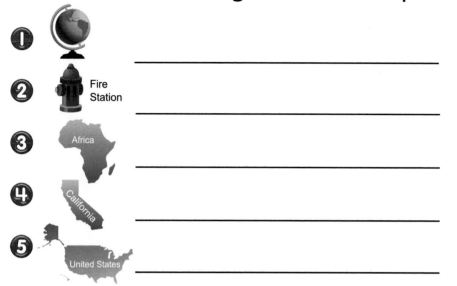

① _____

② Fire Station _____

③ Africa _____

④ California _____

⑤ United States _____

state (p. 59)

country (p. 60)

globe (p. 62)

continent (p. 62)

symbol (p. 68)

Recall Facts

⑥ What does a map show?

⑦ How are models different from pictures and maps?

⑧ What does a map legend show?

⑨ Which would be a good shelter in the cold, snowy mountains?

    A tent   **C** houseboat

    B straw hut   **D** wooden house

⑩ Which is NOT a kind of recreation you would do at the beach?

    A swimming   **C** ice skating

    B volleyball   **D** sailing

Think Critically

⑪ **ANALYSIS SKILL** How are resources in the mountains different from resources at the beach?

⑫ **Make It Relevant** How would your life be different if you lived where it snowed a lot?

Apply Map and Globe Skills

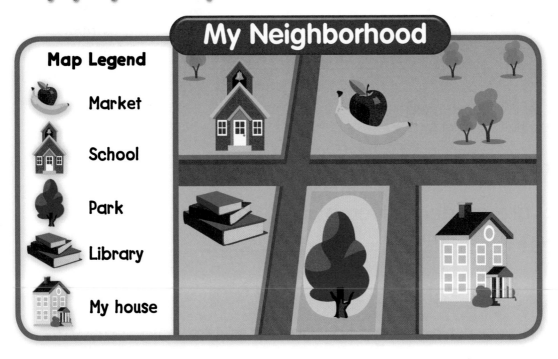

My Neighborhood

Map Legend

🍎 Market

🏫 School

🌳 Park

📚 Library

🏠 My house

⑬ How many places are shown on the map?

⑭ What symbol shows the school?

⑮ Where would you go in this neighborhood to check out a book?

⑯ What is between my house and the library?

Apply Map and Globe Skills

Zoo

17 What is west of the lions?

18 What is north of the elephants?

19 From the tigers, in which direction are the dolphins?

20 Find the gorillas. Now move your finger to the tigers. In which direction did you move?

Activities

Read More

The Sahara
by Lisa Trumbauer

Sun Power
by Susan Ring

The Himalayas
by Susan Ring

Show What You Know

Unit Writing Activity

Tell About a Place
What words could you use to tell a pen pal about where you live?

Write a Letter Write a short letter to your pen pal telling about where you live.

Unit Project

Places We Live Mural
Create a mural to show where you live.

- Think about different things in your community.
- Draw them on a mural.
- Share it with another class.

Visit ACTIVITIES at
www.harcourtschool.com/hss

We Love Our Country

Start with the Standards

1.3 Students know and understand the symbols, icons, and traditions of the United States that provide continuity and a sense of community across time.

The Big Idea

Our Country

We learn about our country through its symbols, heroes, and holidays.

What to Know

✔ What is the Pledge of Allegiance?

✔ Why do we have national holidays?

✔ Why are our country's symbols important?

✔ What are the Declaration of Independence and the United States Constitution?

Show What You Know

★ Unit 3 Test

✎ Writing: A Poem

✏ Unit Project: A Patriotic Party

We Love Our Country

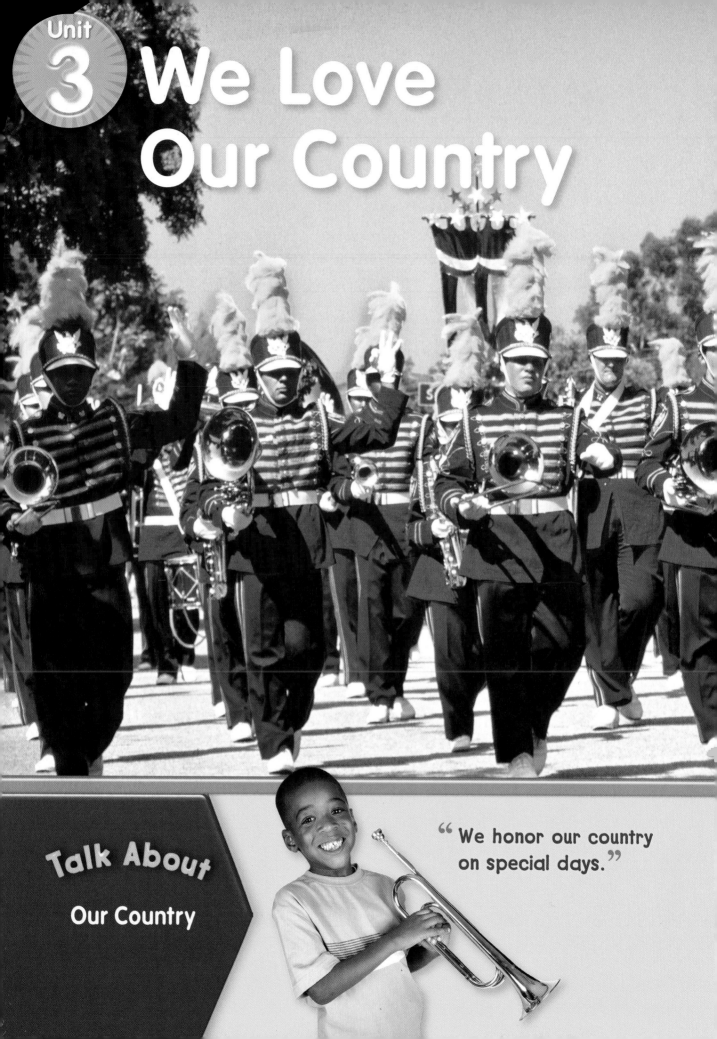

Talk About

Our Country

"We honor our country on special days."

" Our country has many
important symbols. "

" We remember
our heroes. "

97

Preview
Vocabulary

flag A piece of cloth with colors and shapes that stand for things. (page 106)

hero A person who does something brave or important to help others. (page 112)

landmark A symbol that is a place people can visit. (page 122)

national holiday A day to honor a person or an event that is important to our country. (page 113)

freedom The right people have to make their own choices.

(page 129)

GO ONLINE

INTERNET RESOURCES

Go to **www.harcourtschool.com/hss** to view Internet resources for this unit.

Reading Social Studies

Focus Skill

Main Idea and Details

As you read, look for the main idea and details.

● The main idea tells you what you are reading about. It is the most important part.

● A detail gives more information. The details explain the main idea.

Practice the Skill

Read the paragraph.

Main Idea   The United States has many symbols that show that Americans are free. The bald

Detail   eagle is one symbol of our country. It is a strong bird that flies free. We keep the Declaration of Independence and the Constitution of the United States in special places. These symbols show how hard our first leaders worked to make our country free.

Apply What You Learned

Main Idea

The United States has many symbols that show Americans are free.

Details

bald eagle _____ _____

This chart shows the main idea and one detail from what you just read. What details could you add? Copy the chart and fill it in.

Apply as You Read

As you read, look for the main idea and details in each lesson.

Study Skills

Note Taking

Taking notes helps you remember what you read and hear. Notes are important facts and ideas. You can write new facts in a learning log under Note Taking. You can also write what you think about them under Note Making.

Practice the Skill

The learning log on the next page shows what Michael has learned about the Statue of Liberty. Copy the learning log.

- What is written under Note Taking?

- What is written under Note Making?

Learning Log

Note Taking	Note Making
France gave the United States the Statue of Liberty.	That was a big present to give!

Read the paragraph below. Then complete the learning log.

France wanted to give the United States a gift to show that they were friends. The gift was the Statue of Liberty. The statue stands on an island near New York City. People from around the world see the statue and remember that we are free.

Apply as You Read

Make a learning log. As you read this unit, take notes under Note Taking. Add your own ideas and feelings under Note Making.

America

by Samuel F. Smith
illustrated by Erika LeBarre

My country, 'tis of thee,
Sweet land of liberty,
Of thee I sing.
Land where my fathers died,
Land of the Pilgrims' pride,
From every mountainside
Let freedom ring!

My native country, thee,
Land of the noble free,
Thy name I love.
I love thy rocks and rills,
Thy woods and templed hills;
My heart with rapture thrills
Like that above.

Response Corner

1. What does the author tell us about America?

2. **Make It Relevant** How does the song make you feel?

105

What to Know
What is the Pledge of Allegiance?

✓ The American flag is an important symbol of our country.

✓ We say the Pledge of Allegiance to show respect for our flag and our country.

Vocabulary
flag
pledge

Focus Skill **Main Idea and Details**

California Standards
HSS 1.3, 1.3.1

I Pledge Allegiance

The American flag is a symbol of our country. A **flag** is a piece of cloth with colors and shapes that stand for things. States have their own flags. Some groups also have flags.

Our flag is red, white, and blue. It has 50 stars. Each star stands for one of the states in our country. The 13 stripes stand for the first 13 states. Our flag changed as our country grew.

Each morning, we face the flag and say the Pledge of Allegiance. A **pledge** is a kind of promise.

The Pledge of Allegiance

I pledge allegiance to the Flag
of the United States of America,
and to the Republic
for which it stands,
one Nation under God, indivisible,
with liberty and justice for all.

The pledge reminds us about being good citizens. When we say the pledge, we promise to respect the flag and our country.

⚡Fast Fact

In 1814, Francis Scott Key saw a flag still flying after a long battle. He wrote a poem about it called "The Star-Spangled Banner." It is now our country's song. Today the flag that Key saw hangs in a museum.

Summary The Pledge of Allegiance is a promise we make to respect the flag and our country.

Review

1 What is the Pledge of Allegiance?

2 Vocabulary Where have you seen our country's **flag**?

3 Write Write sentences that tell what our country's flag looks like.

4 Main Idea and Details What does the American flag stand for?

Trustworthiness
Respect
Responsibility
Fairness
Caring
Patriotism

Why Character Counts

? **How did Francis Bellamy show his patriotism?**

Francis Bellamy

Francis Bellamy worked for a children's magazine called The Youth's Companion. When Bellamy wrote the Pledge of Allegiance, the magazine published it. On October 11, 1892, schoolchildren said the Pledge for the first time. This day was chosen because it was 400 years from the day Columbus landed in North America.

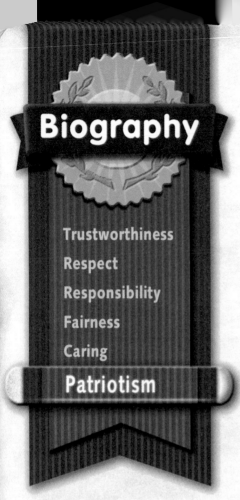

Francis Bellamy wrote the Pledge of Allegiance.

"Let the flag float over every school-house in the land . . ."*

*Francis Bellamy, from a Columbus Day pamphlet, 1892

Bio Brief

1855   1931

Important Dates

1876 Graduates from the University of Rochester

1891 Starts working for the magazine The Youth's Companion

1892 Writes the Pledge of Allegiance

1942 The Pledge of Allegiance becomes the Pledge of our country

Bellamy hoped that the Pledge of Allegiance would help people feel respect for our country and our flag. In 1942, it became the Pledge of our country. Some of the words have changed since then, but in many schools, children still start each day with the Pledge.

GO ONLINE Interactive Multimedia Biographies Visit MULTIMEDIA BIOGRAPHIES at **www.harcourtschool.com/hss**

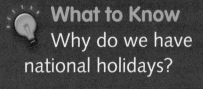

Heroes and Holidays

What to Know
Why do we have national holidays?

✓ Some holidays honor American heroes.

✓ Some holidays honor important events.

Vocabulary
hero
national holiday

 Focus Skill
Main Idea and Details

 California Standards
HSS 1.3, 1.3.2

A **hero** is a person who does something brave or important to help others. Men and women who work in the military are heroes. They help protect our country.

Army

A **national holiday** is a day to honor a person or an event that is important to our country. Memorial Day and Veterans Day are two national holidays. On these days, we remember heroes who have helped in our country's wars.

Navy

Marines

Our country has many heroes. We have holidays to honor them. On Dr. Martin Luther King, Jr., Day, we honor a man who worked to help all Americans have the same rights.

Dr. Martin Luther King, Jr.

Presidents' Day started as George Washington's Birthday. It was a holiday to remember our first President. Now it is a day to remember the work of all our Presidents.

Abraham Lincoln

George Washington

We do special things on national holidays. We have parades, watch fireworks, and get together with family and friends.

Summary National holidays help us remember the important events and heroes of our country.

Review

1. Why do we have national holidays?

2. **Vocabulary** Name an American **hero**.

3. **Activity** With your class, make a chart telling about each of our national holidays.

4. **Focus Skill** **Main Idea and Details** What do Americans do on national holidays?

Read a Calendar

◗ Why It Matters

A **calendar** is used to show time.

◗ What You Need to Know

A calendar shows days, weeks, and months. A week has 7 days. A year has 365 days. It also has 52 weeks and 12 months.

Today means this day. **Yesterday** is the day before today. **Tomorrow** is the day after today.

February

Sunday	Monday	Tuesday	Wednesday	Thursday	Friday	Saturday
				1	2	3
4 Rosa Parks's Birthday	5	6	7	8	9	10
11 Thomas Edison's Birthday	12 Lincoln's Birthday	13	14	15 Susan B. Anthony's Birthday	16	17
18	19 Presidents Day	20	21	22 Washington's Birthday	23	24
25	26	27	28			

❯ Practice the Skill

1 Look at the calendar page. What month does this page show?

2 How many days are there in this month?

3 Name the birthdays in February. On what day of the week is each birthday?

❯ Apply What You Learned

ANALYSIS SKILL Find today, tomorrow, and yesterday on a calendar.

Flag Day

Bernard J. Cigrand was a teacher who lived more than 100 years ago. He loved the American flag. He put it on his desk, where the children in his class could see it. He asked them to write about how the flag made them feel.

Cigrand and others wanted to have a national holiday to honor our flag. They worked for this idea for many years. At last, in 1949, the government made the holiday they wanted. June 14 became Flag Day.

Bernard J. Cigrand

Cigrand taught at Stony Hill School in the state of Wisconsin.

You can see the flag in many places. Some people hang the flag on a flagpole. This is called flying the flag. People fly flags at home and at work. The flag flies at your school, too.

Sometimes, people fly the flag halfway between the top and the bottom of the flagpole. They do this when someone important has died. Flying the flag this way shows respect for the person.

Did You Know?

Did you know that there are rules for how to treat the flag?

★ Never let the flag touch the ground.
★ Raise the flag quickly. Lower it slowly.
★ Do not use the flag on clothing, towels, napkins, or plates.

Think About It!

Make It Relevant How do you feel about the flag?

American Symbols

The United States of America has many symbols. These symbols stand for events, people, and ideas that are important to us.

What to Know

Why are our country's symbols important?

✔ Our country has many symbols.

✔ Some of our symbols are landmarks.

Vocabulary
landmark

Focus Skill
Main Idea and Details

California Standards
HSS 1.3, 1.3.3

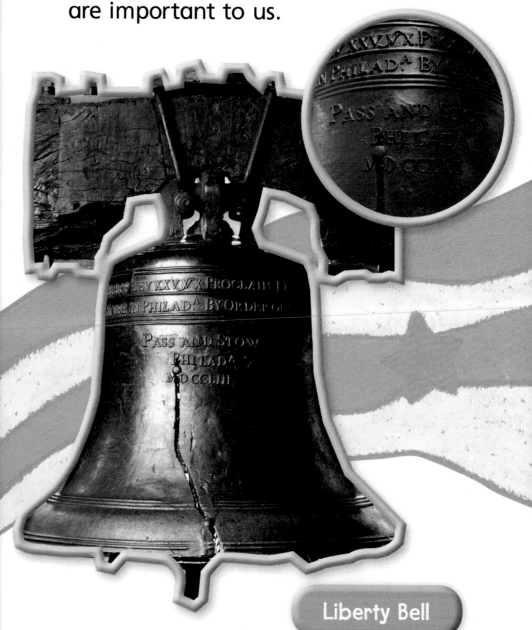

Liberty Bell

Some symbols are plants or animals. The rose and the bald eagle are American symbols.

Symbols can also be objects. Our country's flag is a symbol. The pictures on our money are symbols, too.

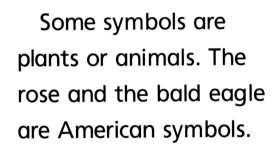

Bald Eagle

Some symbols are places that we can visit. These symbols are called **landmarks**.

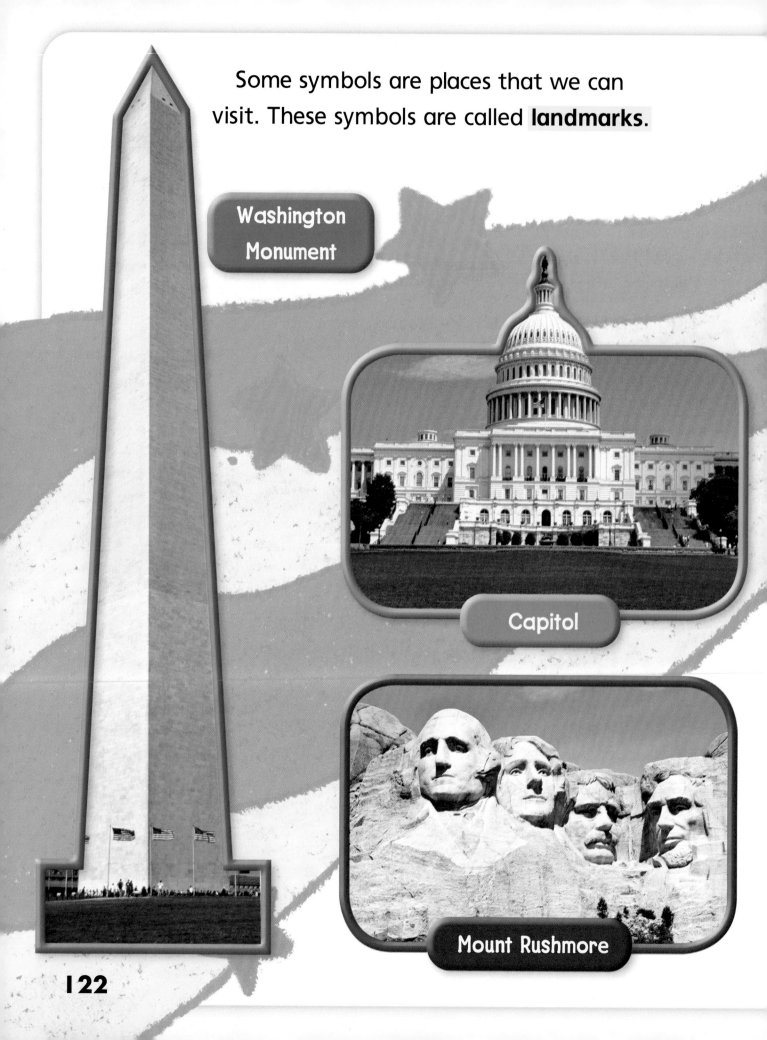

Washington Monument

Capitol

Mount Rushmore

Moving to America

Long ago, many families from other countries sailed across the ocean to make new homes in the United States. Imagine how the children felt! When they sailed into New York Harbor, the first thing they saw was a giant statue. One boy from Germany said, "I thought she was one of the seven wonders of the world." *

*The American Park Network

Statue of Liberty

Summary Our country has symbols that stand for people, events, and ideas that are important to us.

Review

1. Why are our country's symbols important?

2. **Vocabulary** What is one **landmark** in our country?

3. **Activity** Make a mobile that shows some of our country's symbols.

4. **Main Idea and Details** What bird is an American symbol?

123

Read a Diagram

❯ Why It Matters

A **diagram** is a picture that shows the parts of something.

❯ What You Need to Know

The picture on the next page is a diagram of the Statue of Liberty. The statue shows a woman who stands for freedom.

❯ Practice the Skill

1 What is the woman holding up high?

2 How many windows are in her crown?

3 What is the woman wearing?

4 What is the name of the island the statue is on?

124

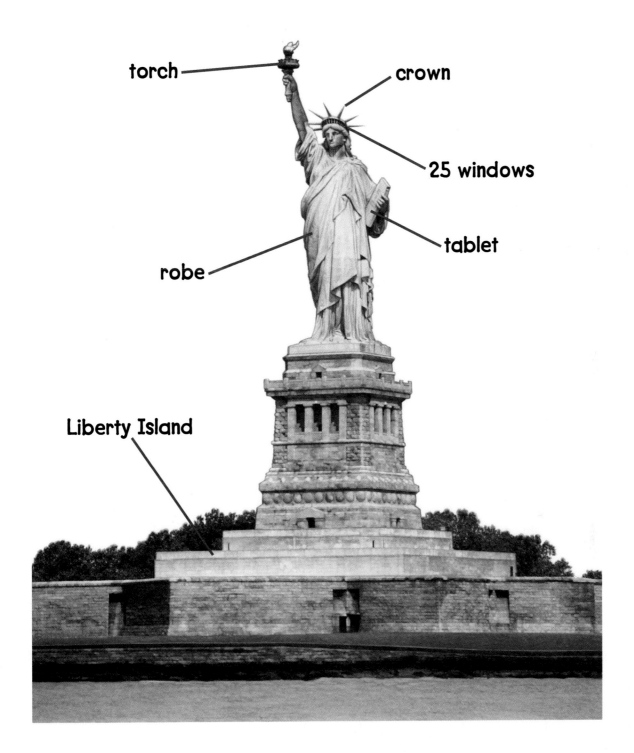

torch

crown

25 windows

tablet

robe

Liberty Island

❯ Apply What You Learned

Make a diagram of another American
landmark or symbol. Name the parts.

What to Know
What are the Declaration of Independence and the United States Constitution?

✓ Settlers came to North America from Europe.

✓ Settlers wanted their freedom.

Vocabulary
settler
colony
freedom

Focus Skill Main Idea and Details

California Standards
HSS 1.3, 1.3.3

Our Country Begins

More than three hundred years ago, settlers sailed to North America from countries in Europe. A **settler** is a person who makes a home in a new place.

ANALYSIS SKILL What ocean did the Mayflower cross?

The 13 Colonies

England had 13 colonies in the eastern part of North America. These colonies became the first 13 states of the United States of America.

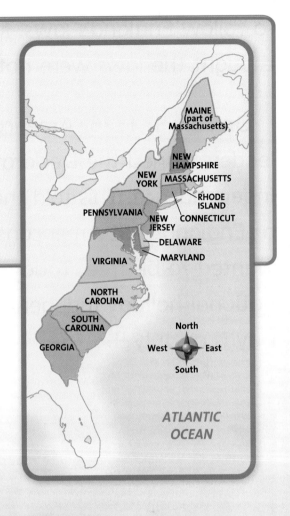

MAINE
(part of Massachusetts)

NEW HAMPSHIRE

NEW YORK   MASSACHUSETTS

RHODE ISLAND

PENNSYLVANIA   CONNECTICUT

NEW JERSEY

DELAWARE

MARYLAND

VIRGINIA

NORTH CAROLINA

SOUTH CAROLINA

GEORGIA

North
West   East
South

ATLANTIC OCEAN

Many of the settlers were from England. The English king called their land a **colony** of England. This meant that the land was ruled by England.

The people living in the colonies had to follow England's laws. Many people thought the laws were not fair.

On July 4, 1776, American leaders signed the Declaration of Independence. This told the king of England that Americans wanted to be free. Today, the national holiday Independence Day is on July 4.

"Where liberty is, there is my country."
—Benjamin Franklin

from a letter to Benjamin Vaughn, March 14, 1783

Americans had to fight a war with England for their **freedom**, or the right to make choices. The Americans won the war. Then American leaders wrote the United States Constitution. The Constitution is the set of rules for our country.

Marching drum

Summary The Declaration of Independence and the United States Constitution are important symbols of our freedom.

Review

❶ 💡 What are the Declaration of Independence and the United States Constitution?

❷ **Vocabulary** Why does a **settler** move to a new country?

❸ ✏️ **Write** Explain why American leaders wrote the Constitution.

❹ (Focus Skill) **Main Idea and Details** Why is July 4 important?

129

Primary Sources

Learning About Freedom

You can learn about the birth of our country from things that were made at that time. Maps, papers, and works of art show the ideas and feelings people had when they were starting the United States of America.

Painting of John Adams, 1800s

❶ What can you learn by reading someone's journal?

A page from John Adams's journal, 1776

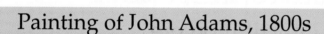

130

② What do this map and this drawing tell you about our country long ago?

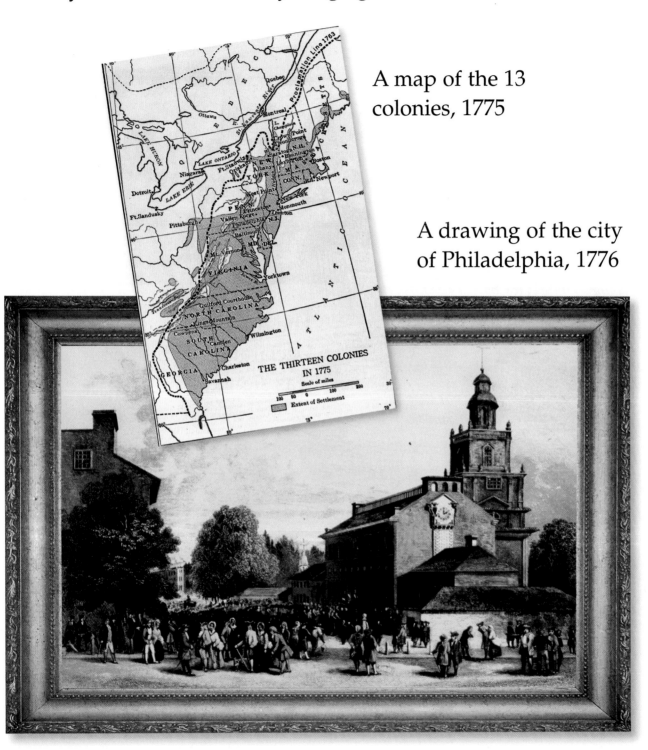

A map of the 13 colonies, 1775

A drawing of the city of Philadelphia, 1776

3 What do the names at the bottom of the Declaration of Independence tell you?

The Declaration of Independence

The room where the Declaration of Independence was signed

Pen and ink set used by the signers

132

4 What do the words "We the People . . ." tell you about the rules and laws in the Constitution?

The United States Constitution

George Washington helped write the Constitution

ANALYSIS SKILL **Analyze Primary Sources**
Make It Relevant Find a photo, paper, or object from your family's history. Write a few sentences telling why it is important to your family.

Visit PRIMARY SOURCES at
www.harcourtschool.com/hss

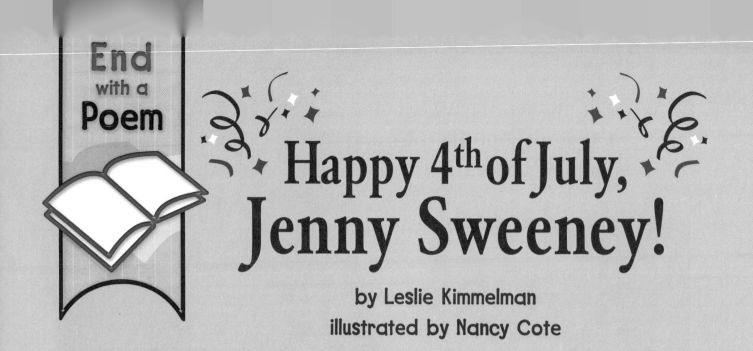

Happy 4th of July, Jenny Sweeney!

by Leslie Kimmelman
illustrated by Nancy Cote

Sun's up high, Fourth of July!

Lots of preparation for a day of celebration.

Jenny Sweeney washes Rags.

Mrs. Berger hangs up flags.

Fireman Mike scrubs down his truck.

Quentin has beginner's luck.

The Dalal family smiles proudly.

"We're Americans now!" they

proclaim loudly.

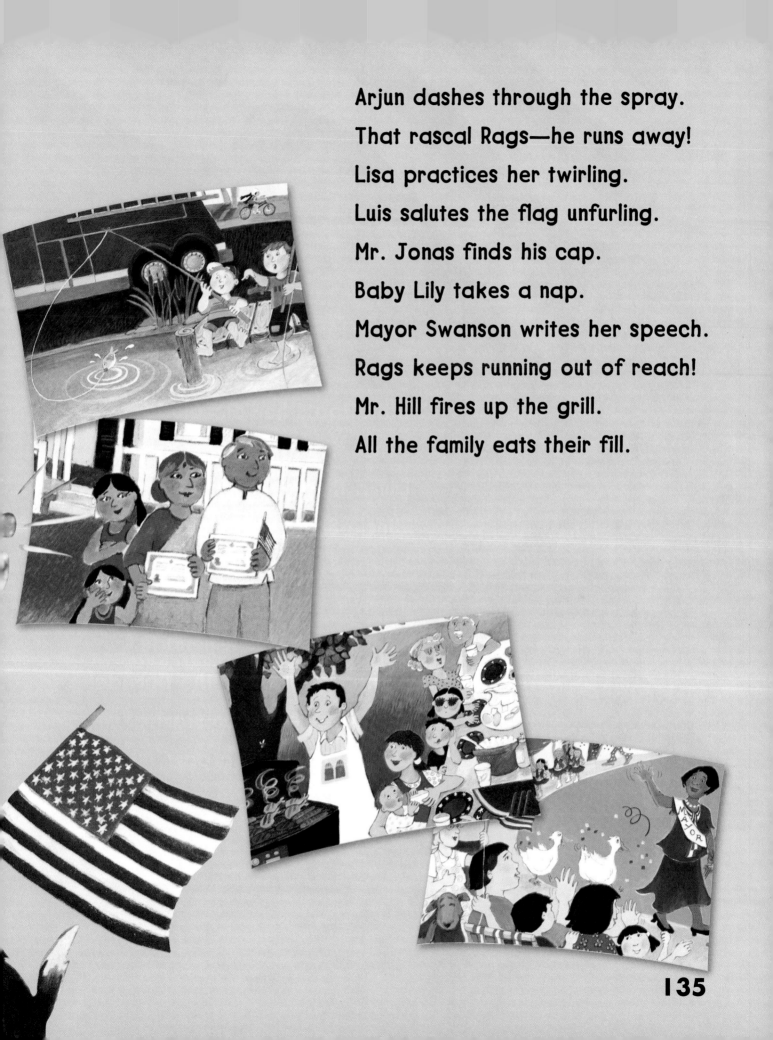

Arjun dashes through the spray.

That rascal Rags—he runs away!

Lisa practices her twirling.

Luis salutes the flag unfurling.

Mr. Jonas finds his cap.

Baby Lily takes a nap.

Mayor Swanson writes her speech.

Rags keeps running out of reach!

Mr. Hill fires up the grill.

All the family eats their fill.

Katie toots her piccolo.
Jenny ties a big red bow.
Emma finishes her float:
"Uncle Sam Wants You to Vote!"
Mayor Swanson tests the mike.
Jenny's ready on her bike.
Jimmy Yang sips lemonade.
Look! It's time for the parade!
Let the celebration start!
Everybody plays a part.

Gladly, proudly, down the street,
joyful music, marching feet.
Fireworks light up the dark
as Jenny watches in the park.
What a party!
What a day—

Happy Birthday, U.S.A.!

Response Corner

1   What kinds of things are people in this poem doing to honor the Fourth of July?

2   **Make It Relevant**   Write a few sentences to tell what your family does on the Fourth of July.

How Communities Honor Their Citizens

Get Ready

Many communities honor people who have done something important. They may name a street, park, or building for such a person.

Locate It
California

Big Sur

Santa Ana   Riverside

What to See

King High School in Riverside, California, is named for Dr. Martin Luther King, Jr. He is a national hero who helped get the same rights for all Americans.

Julia Pfeiffer Burns State Park is named for a woman who helped settle the Big Sur area of California in the early 1900s. This point was one of her favorite spots.

California citizen Ronald W. Reagan was the 40th President of the United States. This courthouse in Santa Ana is named to honor him.

A Virtual Tour

GO ONLINE Visit VIRTUAL TOURS at www.harcourtschool.com/hss

💡 **Our Country** We learn about our country through its symbols, heroes, and holidays.

⭐ (Focus Skill) Main Idea and Details

Copy and fill in the chart to show what you learned about the Pledge of Allegiance.

Main Idea

The Pledge of Allegiance reminds us about being good citizens.

⬆

Details

We face the flag when we say the pledge.

_____

_____

140

Use Vocabulary

Write the word that completes each sentence.

1. The Washington Monument is a _____.

2. The Fourth of July is a _____.

3. The red and white stripes on our _____ stand for the first thirteen states.

4. Americans fought a war with England to have _____, or the right to make choices.

5. Dr. Martin Luther King, Jr., is a _____.

flag
(p. 106)
hero
(p. 112)
national holiday
(p. 113)
landmark
(p. 122)
freedom
(p. 129)

Recall Facts

6. What do the 50 stars on the American flag stand for?

7. Why do we have Veterans Day?

8. What flower is an American symbol?

9. Which of these symbols is a landmark?
   A flag   C rose
   B Mount Rushmore D bald eagle

10. How many states did the United States of America have at first?
    A 10   C 13
    B 5   D 50

Think Critically

11 **ANALYSIS SKILL** Why did Americans fight to be free from England?

12 **Make It Relevant** How would your life be different if we did not have the United States Constitution?

Apply Chart and Graph Skills

13 How many days are in January?

14 When do we honor Dr. Martin Luther King, Jr.?

15 What is special about January 1?

16 On what day of the week is Gold Discovery Day?

Apply Chart and Graph Skills

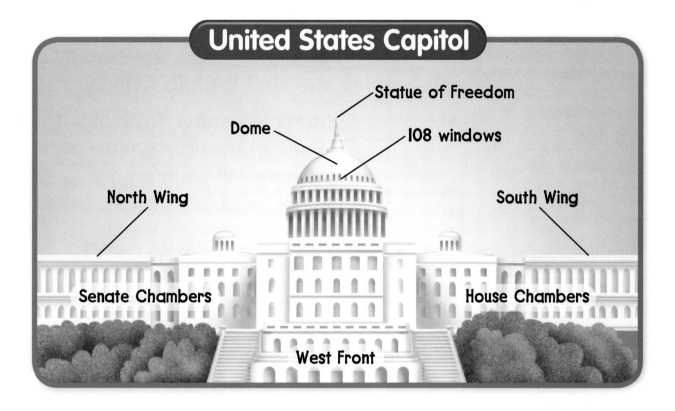

United States Capitol

Statue of Freedom

Dome

108 windows

North Wing

South Wing

Senate Chambers

House Chambers

West Front

⑰ What is on top of the dome?

⑱ What is the front of the Capitol building called?

⑲ How many windows are in the dome?

⑳ Which chambers are in the South Wing?

Show What You Know

Read More

Fourth of July
by Alan M.
Ruben

**Philadelphia:
Home of
Liberty**
by Lisa
Trumbauer

**Visit the
Capitol**
by Lisa
Trumbauer

Unit Writing Activity

Choose a Symbol Think about a famous American symbol or landmark. Why is it a good symbol for our country?

Write a Poem Write a poem about the symbol or landmark.

Unit Project

Patriotic Party Plan a patriotic party.

- Plan to tell about an American hero, holiday, symbol, or landmark.
- Make invitations and classroom decorations.
- Hold the party.

GO ONLINE Visit ACTIVITIES at www.harcourtschool.com/hss

Our Changing World

 Start with the Standards

1.4 Students compare and contrast everyday life in different times and places around the world and recognize that some aspects of people, places, and things change over time while others stay the same.

The Big Idea

Change

In many ways, people today are the same as people who lived long ago. But the way people live has changed over time.

What to Know

 What were schools like long ago?

✔ What can happen to communities over time?

✔ How has transportation changed over time?

✔ How are the lives of people today different from the lives of people in the past? How are they the same?

Show What You Know

★ Unit 4 Test

✎ Writing: A Story

✏ Unit Project: A "Then and Now" Scrapbook

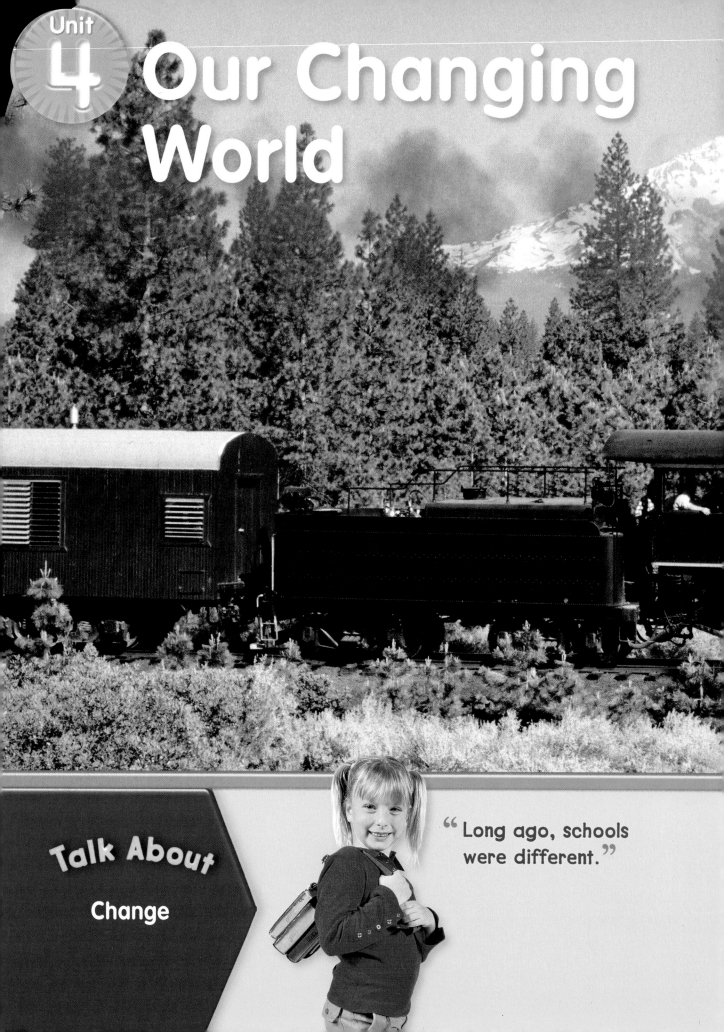

Unit 4 Our Changing World

Talk About

Change

"Long ago, schools were different."

"The tools we use have changed over time."

"Technology has made transportation better."

past   The time before now.

(page 166)

present   The time now.

(page 167)

change To become different. (page 158)

time line A line that shows the order in which things have happened. (page 170)

technology All of the tools we use to make our lives easier. (page 176)

GO ONLINE INTERNET RESOURCES

Go to **www.harcourtschool.com/hss** to view Internet resources for this unit.

147

Reading Social Studies

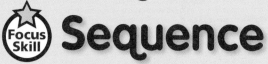

(Focus Skill) Sequence

As you read, think about sequence.

● Sequence is the order in which things happen. What happens first? What happens next? What happens last?

● Look for sequence words such as <u>first</u>, <u>next</u>, <u>then</u>, <u>later</u>, <u>last</u>, and <u>finally</u>.

Practice the Skill

Read the paragraph.

Long ago, the school day was not like your school day. Children walked to school. All the (Sequence) grades shared one classroom. First, they all read out loud. Next, each grade was called up for a lesson while the other children worked quietly. Last, the children helped the teacher do chores. They cleaned the classroom and got wood for the fire. When school was over, the children walked home.

First — All the grades read out loud.

Next

Last

This chart shows the sequence of things that happened on a school day long ago. Copy the chart and fill in the next things in order.

Apply as You Read

As you read, look for words that tell the sequence of things.

Study Skills

Use Visuals

Looking at pictures makes it easier to understand what you are reading about. Pictures also make what you are reading about more interesting.

Practice the Skill

Pictures can tell a story. Sometimes pictures have captions, or words that tell about them. Look at the pictures on these pages. Ask questions about what you see.

Family life long ago.

- What are the people doing?

- How are their clothes like your clothes? How are their clothes different?

- How is their home like your home? How is it different?

- What do these pictures tell you about how life has changed?

Apply as You Read

As you read this unit, look closely at the pictures to learn what things were like long ago. Think about how pictures help you understand what you read.

Children of Long Ago

by Lessie Jones Little

illustrated by Jan Spivey Gilchrist

PART I

The children who lived a long time ago
In little country towns
Ate picnics under spreading trees,
Played hopscotch on the cool dirt yards,
Picked juicy grapes from broad grapevines,
Pulled beets and potatoes from the ground,
Those children of long ago.

The children who lived a long time ago
In little country towns
Tromped to school on hard-frozen roads,
Warmed themselves by wood-burning stoves,
Ate supper by light from oil-filled lamps,
Built fancy snowmen dressed like clowns,
Those children of long ago.

The children who lived a long time ago
In little country towns
Decked themselves in their Sunday best,
Went to church and visited friends,
Sang happy songs with their mamas and papas,
Traveled through books for sights and sounds,
Those children of long ago.

PART II

Sometimes sad and sorry,
Sometimes jolly and glad,
> They cried,
> They laughed,
> They worked,
> They played,
> They learned,
> They loved,
Those children of long ago.

Response Corner

1 What kinds of things did the children in this poem do long ago?

2 **Make It Relevant** How are the children in this poem like you? How are they different?

What to Know
What were schools like long ago?

✓ Schools have changed over time.

✓ In some ways, schools today are the same as schools long ago.

Vocabulary
change
tool

Focus Skill **Sequence**

 California Standards
HSS 1.4, 1.4.1

Schools Long Ago

Schools, like other things, change over time. To **change** is to become different.

Long ago, many children learned at home. Others went to schools that had only one room and one teacher. Children of all ages learned together.

One-room school, 1917

Today, children go to many kinds of schools. Most schools have many rooms and many teachers. Some ways of learning are the same as in schools long ago. Some ways are different.

Special-needs school

Public school

Home school

We have many tools to help us learn. A **tool** is something that people use to do work. In schools long ago, children had tools that were different from tools we have today.

lunch pail, late 1800s

School Tools of Long Ago

Long ago, children learned to read from a hornbook. They used chalk to write on small chalkboards called slates. They dipped pens in ink to write on paper. Children used a tool called an abacus for counting. Which tools look like things you use today?

hornbook

abacus

slate

pen and ink

Long ago, children played many of the same games children play today. They played different games, too. Most of their toys were made by hand.

ANALYSIS SKILL Look at these two pictures of children playing games long ago. Which game looks like one that is still played today?

Children in History

George S. Parker

George S. Parker was good at thinking up new games. In 1883, he sold his first game when he was only 16 years old. He asked his brothers to help. Their company made many popular board games that we still play today.

GAME of BANKING

Long ago, some children had to walk miles to get to school. Others rode in wagons. Today, children ride to school in cars or school buses. They also walk to school, as children did long ago.

Summary Schools long ago were different from schools today. In some ways, they were the same.

Review

1. What were schools like long ago?

2. **Vocabulary** What are some **tools** children used in school long ago? What tools do you use today?

3. **Write** Draw a picture of a school of long ago. Write a sentence to tell about it.

4. **Focus Skill** **Sequence** What writing tools did children use before there were pencils and pens like the ones we use today?

Put Things in Groups

❯ Why It Matters

You can put things in groups to see how they are the same and how they are different.

❯ What You Need to Know

A **table** is a chart that shows things in groups. This table has two groups. One group shows tools of long ago. The other shows tools we use today.

❯ Practice the Skill

❶ Which side of the table shows tools children use today?

❷ When did children write on slates? How do you know?

❸ Did children use markers long ago? How does the table show this?

School Tools	
Long Ago	Today

🌙 Apply What You Learned

Make It Relevant   Make a table. On one side, show tools you would use to make a picture. On the other side, show tools you would use to write a story.

What to Know
What can happen to communities over time?

✔ Communities are always changing.

✔ People help change communities.

Vocabulary
past
present
future

Sequence

California Standards
HSS 1.4, 1.4.1

Communities in the Past

Places grow and change over time just as people do. Marc lives in Julian, California. This is what his community looked like in the **past**, or the time before now.

Past

Marc's community has changed a lot. This is what Julian looks like in the **present**, or the time now.

Communities change in many ways. People can help change them. Many years ago, families started to move to Julian. They built homes, schools, and stores. Julian grew bigger.

Present

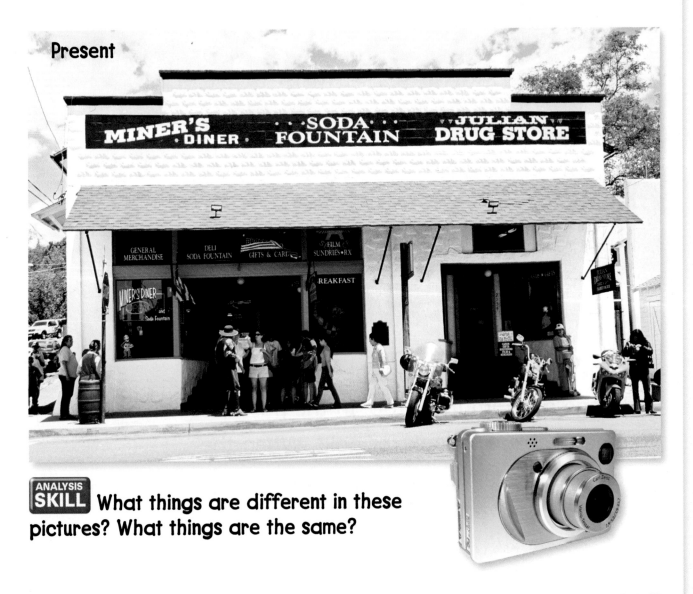

ANALYSIS SKILL What things are different in these pictures? What things are the same?

The kinds of work that people do can change a community, too. In the past, people came to Julian to look for gold. When the gold was gone, people needed new jobs.

Now Julian is known for growing apples. Julian will keep changing in the **future**, or the time to come.

Summary Communities change over time. People help change communities.

Summary Communities change over time. People help change communities.

Review

1. What can happen to communities over time?

2. **Vocabulary** How was Marc's community different in the **past**?

3. **Activity** Draw a picture to show how your community may have looked in the past.

4. **Sequence** What did Marc's community become known for after the gold was gone?

Use a Time Line

❱ Why It Matters

You can show how things change over time.

❱ What You Need to Know

A **time line** shows the order in which things have happened. A time line can show days, weeks, months, or years. You read a time line from left to right. The things that happened first are on the left.

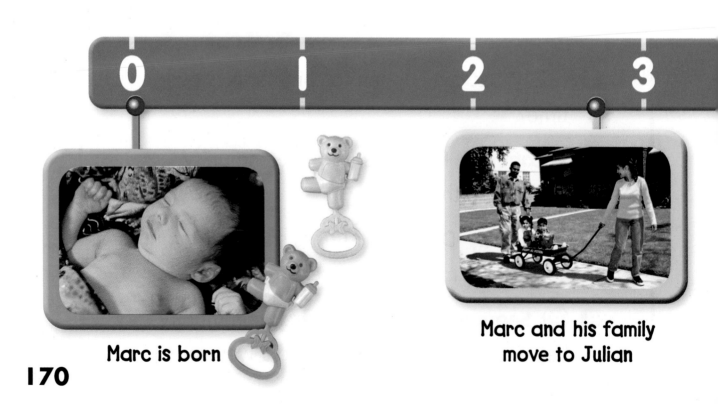

0   1   2   3

Marc is born

Marc and his family move to Julian

➤ Practice the Skill

① Look at Marc's time line. How old was Marc when he started school?

② Find when Marc was six. Which picture shows this?

③ What happened when Marc was almost three years old?

➤ Apply What You Learned

ANALYSIS SKILL Make It Relevant   Make a time line to show how you have changed.

Marc's first bike

Marc starts school

Marc's seventh birthday party

17

Learning Through Storytelling

Stories about the past can tell us how things have changed over time. At a theater called Stagebridge in Oakland, California, children hear stories from older adults.

People at the theater also teach children how to tell stories. First, the children ask grandparents or older people in their family to share stories about the past. Next, they write the stories down on paper. Then, the children share the stories with people in their community.

Older citizens can tell us about the past.

You can find out many things when you listen to older people tell stories. Their stories can tell you what life was like long ago. The stories show you how some things have changed and how some things have stayed the same.

Children share stories, too.

Did You Know?

Did you know that you can tell a story like this?

★ Ask an older person in your family what life was like when he or she was your age.

★ Write down the story. Ask questions to find out more.

★ Tell the story to others.

Think About It!

Make It Relevant Who could you ask to tell a story about the past?

What to Know
How has transportation changed over time?

✓ New technology has changed transportation.

✓ New kinds of transportation have changed the way we live.

Vocabulary
technology

Focus Skill Sequence

California Standards
HSS 1.4, 1.4.2

Changes in Transportation

In the past, transportation was very slow. It took a long time for people to go places.

canoe

174

Most people did not take trips to see new places. Many never went far from where they were born.

covered wagon

⚡Fast Fact

Long ago, mail was carried from the state of Missouri to California by the Pony Express. Riders on horses made the trip in only ten days. That was express—very fast—service then!

People have used technology
to make new ways to go places.
Technology is all of the tools we use
to make our lives easier.

Technology has helped transportation in many ways. Boats, trains, cars, planes, and other kinds of transportation are now safer and faster.

Technology is always changing. Today, people can easily go to places that are far away. They can take a trip around the world in just a few days. People have even gone into space. Transportation has changed a lot!

Depart: Earth

Arrive: Moon

Summary Transportation has changed. Technology has made transportation better now than it was long ago.

Review

1. 💡 How has transportation changed over time?

2. **Vocabulary** How has **technology** changed transportation?

3. 🖌 **Activity** Make a chart like the one on page 165 to show transportation long ago and today.

4. (Focus Skill) **Sequence** Which of these kinds of transportation came first—the airplane, the car, or the canoe?

Tell Fact from Fiction

❱ Why It Matters

Some stories are made up, and some stories are about real things.

❱ What You Need to Know

Stories about real things are **nonfiction**. These stories tell only facts. A **fact** is something that is true and not made up.

Stories that are mostly made up are **fiction**. Some stories that are fiction have facts in them to make them seem real.

Sometimes I am up.

Sometimes I am down.

Practice the Skill

1. Look at these two books. They both show a kind of transportation.

2. Look at the pictures and the words in each book.

3. Which book is fiction? Which book has only facts?

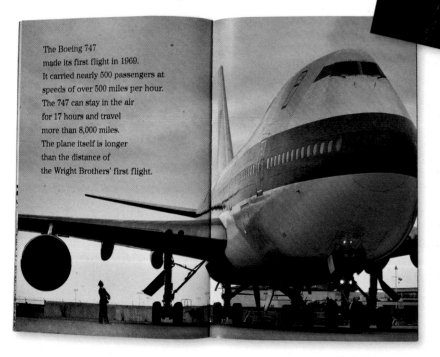

The Boeing 747 made its first flight in 1969. It carried nearly 500 passengers at speeds of over 500 miles per hour. The 747 can stay in the air for 17 hours and travel more than 8,000 miles. The plane itself is longer than the distance of the Wright Brothers' first flight.

Apply What You Learned

ANALYSIS SKILL Find a book about the past. Do you think it is fiction or nonfiction? How can you tell?

Trustworthiness

Respect

Responsibility

Fairness

Caring

Patriotism

Why Character Counts

❓ How did Bessie Coleman show respect for herself and others?

Bessie Coleman was the first African American woman to become a pilot.

Bessie Coleman

Becoming the first African American woman pilot was not easy for Bessie Coleman. American flying schools would not let her in. In the early 1900s, there had never been an African American woman pilot. "I refused to take no for an answer,"* she wrote.

*attributed to Bessie Coleman, 1921

In 1995, Bessie Coleman was honored with this stamp.

Bessie Coleman learned French to take flying lessons in France.

Coleman went to a flying school in France. She became the first American woman—and the first African American— to get an international pilot's license. She came home famous.

At one flying show, there were two gates at the airport. One was for black people, and one was for white people. Coleman would not fly until everyone could use the same gate. Bessie Coleman helped many people learn to respect one another.

Bio Brief

1892   1926

Important Dates

1918 Pilots' stories make her want to learn to fly

1920 Goes to flying school in France

1921 Gets her international pilot's license

1922 People cheer at her first air show

Interactive Multimedia Biographies
Visit MULTIMEDIA BIOGRAPHIES
at **www.harcourtschool.com/hss**

4 People in the Past

What to Know

How are the lives of people today different from the lives of people in the past? How are they the same?

✔ Life has changed from the way it was in the past.

✔ Technology has changed the way we do many things.

Vocabulary
communication

Focus Skill Sequence

California Standards
HSS 1.4, 1.4.3

Darla loves to watch home movies with Grandma Mary. Darla learns what life was like when Grandma Mary was a child.

The movies show how people dressed then. "I always wore dresses when I was a little girl," Grandma Mary explains. Darla thinks Grandma Mary looked pretty, but Darla likes to wear jeans and T-shirts.

"Like many other women back then, my mother worked at home," Grandma Mary tells Darla. "She took care of our house and my brothers and me."

Today, both men and women work at home. Men and women also have jobs outside the home. Grandma Mary works as a dentist.

Grandma Mary tells Darla about the fun she had as a little girl. Some of the games she played were different from Darla's games. Some were the same.

"Every year, our family went to the Old Spanish Days festival in Santa Barbara, California," Grandma Mary says. "People still go to it today."

Every day, people talk and write to share ideas and feelings. This sharing is called **communication**.

In the past, Grandma Mary wrote letters to her friends and talked to people on the telephone.

Today, she and Darla communicate in the same ways as in the past. They also send letters and pictures by e-mail on the computer.

Summary Some things people do have stayed the same over time. Other things people do have changed.

Review

1.  How are the lives of people today different from the lives of people in the past? How are they the same?

2. **Vocabulary** What kinds of **communication** did people use in the past to share news?

3. **Write** Ask an older person in your family what life was like in the past. Write down what he or she says. Share it with your class.

4. **Sequence** Was Grandma Mary a little girl before or after Darla was born?

Home Tools

Tools help us do things. People have used different kinds of tools in their homes for many years. New technology makes tools better. Look at these tools that people used long ago to see how home tools have changed over time.

milkman, 1940s

❶ What do you think it was like to use these tools?

refrigerator, 1930s

potato masher

eggbeater

190

2 How are these tools like tools you have
at home today?

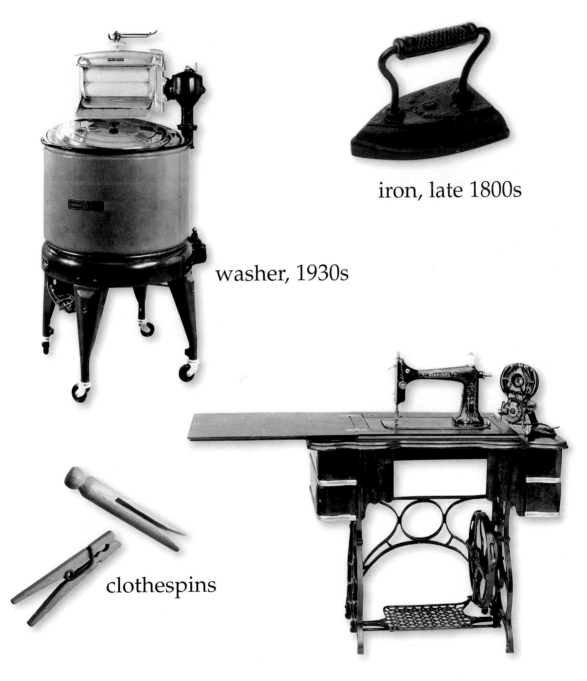

washer, 1930s

iron, late 1800s

clothespins

sewing machine, late 1800s

❸ How are these tools different from ones that you use?

typewriter, 1920s

telephone, early 1900s

radio, 1920s

camera, early 1900s

phonograph, late 1800s

television, 1950s

ANALYSIS SKILL **Analyze Primary Sources**

Look at the pictures again. Then think about tools we use today. Write a sentence that tells how you think tools have changed.

GO ONLINE

Visit PRIMARY SOURCES at
www.harcourtschool.com/hss

"Quilts"
Cherry Pies and Lullabies

by Lynn Reiser

In this story, a person from one generation makes a quilt for someone of the next generation. A generation is a group of people who are born and live at the same time. Some things are different in each generation. Some things are the same.

My great-grandmother
gave a quilt
to my grandmother;

my grandmother
gave a quilt
to my mother;

my mother
gave a quilt
to me;

and
I gave a quilt
to my bear.

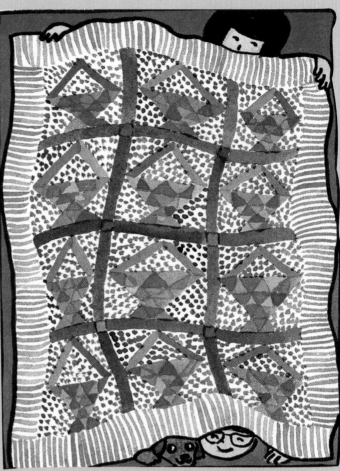

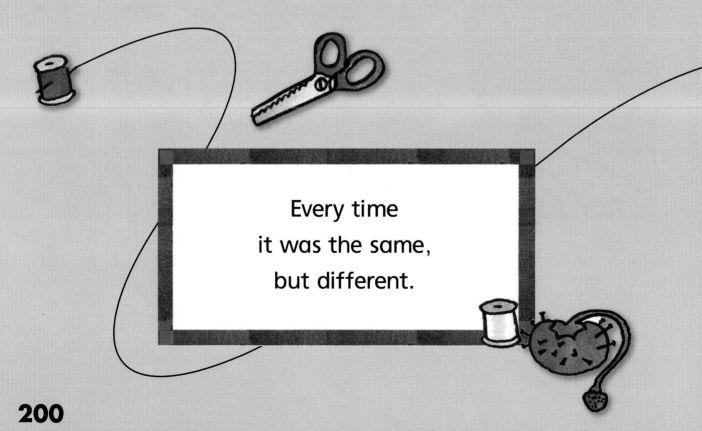

Every time
it was the same,
but different.

Response Corner

1. What was the same about each generation in this story? What was different?

2. **Make It Relevant** Tell about something your family has passed from generation to generation.

Columbia
State Historic Park

Get Ready

Long ago, people came to the town of Columbia in California to look for gold. Today the town is a state historic park. People visit to see what life was like during the Gold Rush.

Locate It
California

Columbia

What to See

Visitors to Columbia learn how to pan for gold.

The town's first bank still looks the same as it did in the 1850s.

Inside the Engine Company is an old fire engine used to put out fires long ago.

An early elementary school

Visitors get around by walking or riding a stagecoach just as people did long ago.

A Virtual Tour

GO ONLINE

Visit VIRTUAL TOURS at www.harcourtschool.com/hss

Review

💡 **Change** In many ways, people today are the same as people who lived long ago. But the way people live has changed over time.

⭐ (Focus Skill) **Sequence**

Copy and fill in the chart to show what you learned about how transportation has changed.

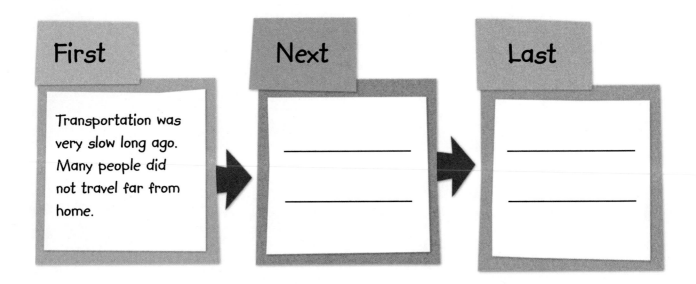

First

Transportation was very slow long ago. Many people did not travel far from home.

Next

_____

_____

Last

_____

_____

Use Vocabulary

Fill in the blanks with the correct words.

Maria made a ❶ _____ to show the order in which things have happened in her town. She learned how people lived in the ❷ _____, or the time before now. She also showed how people live now, in the ❸ _____. Maria learned how things ❹ _____, or become different. One change is that people now use cars instead of horses. Cars are one kind of ❺ _____ that makes our lives easier.

change
(p. 158)

past
(p. 166)

present
(p. 167)

time line
(p. 170)

technology
(p. 176)

Recall Facts

❻ How did children get to school long ago?

❼ Name two things that change a community.

❽ How has technology helped transportation?

❾ Why might people talk or write to each other?
- A to share ideas and feelings
- B to be alone
- C to get more rest
- D to act fairly

❿ Which of these statements was NOT true long ago?
- A People live in communities.
- B Games are fun.
- C People use e-mail.
- D Children go to school.

Think Critically

11 **ANALYSIS SKILL** How might our world change in the future?

12 **Make It Relevant** How has your community changed over time?

Apply Chart and Graph Skills

13 Which side of the table shows transportation that we use in the present?

14 Did people fly in big jets in the past? How can you tell?

15 When did people travel on large ships with sails?

16 On which side of the table would you add a space shuttle?

Transportation	
Past	Present

Apply Chart and Graph Skills

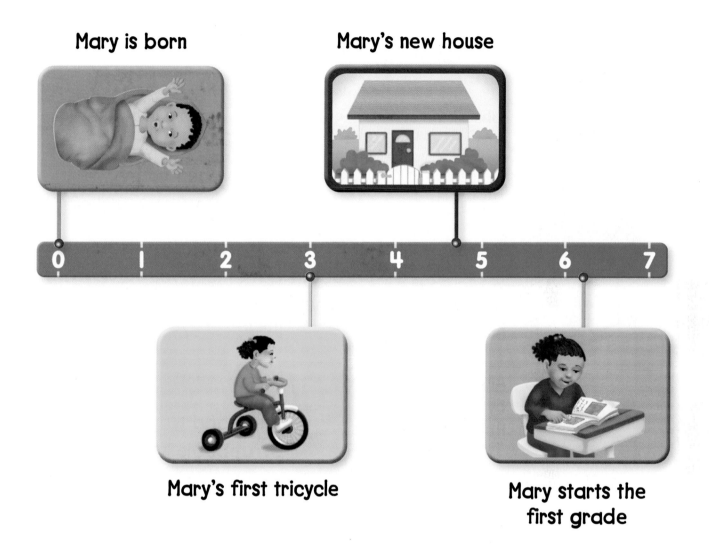

Mary is born

Mary's new house

Mary's first tricycle

Mary starts the first grade

0 1 2 3 4 5 6 7

⑰ What does this time line show?

⑱ When did Mary get her first tricycle?

⑲ What happened when Mary was almost five?

⑳ What happened last on this time line?

Activities

Read More

Jobs of the Past by Jeri Cipriano

The Wright Brothers and the First Airplane by Alan M. Ruben

San Diego by Sheila Sweeny

Show What You Know

Unit Writing Activity

Share a Memory All things change. People change, too. Think about when you were younger. What were you like?

Write a Story Write a story about a memory you have from when you were younger.

Unit Project

Then and Now Scrapbook Make a past and present scrapbook.

- Draw or find pictures of life in the past and now.
- Paste the pictures on pages.
- Share your scrapbook.

 Visit ACTIVITIES at **www.harcourtschool.com/hss**

All About People

 Start with the Standards

1.5 Students describe the human characteristics of familiar places and the varied backgrounds of American citizens and residents in those places.

The Big Idea

People

Although Americans may come from different backgrounds, they share some beliefs.

What to Know

✔ Who belongs to a community?

✔ How have American Indians affected our culture?

✔ How have immigrants added to our culture?

✔ What can folktales tell you about cultures?

✔ How do people show their cultures?

Show What You Know

★ Unit 5 Test

✎ Writing: A Paragraph

🖌 Unit Project: A Culture Fair

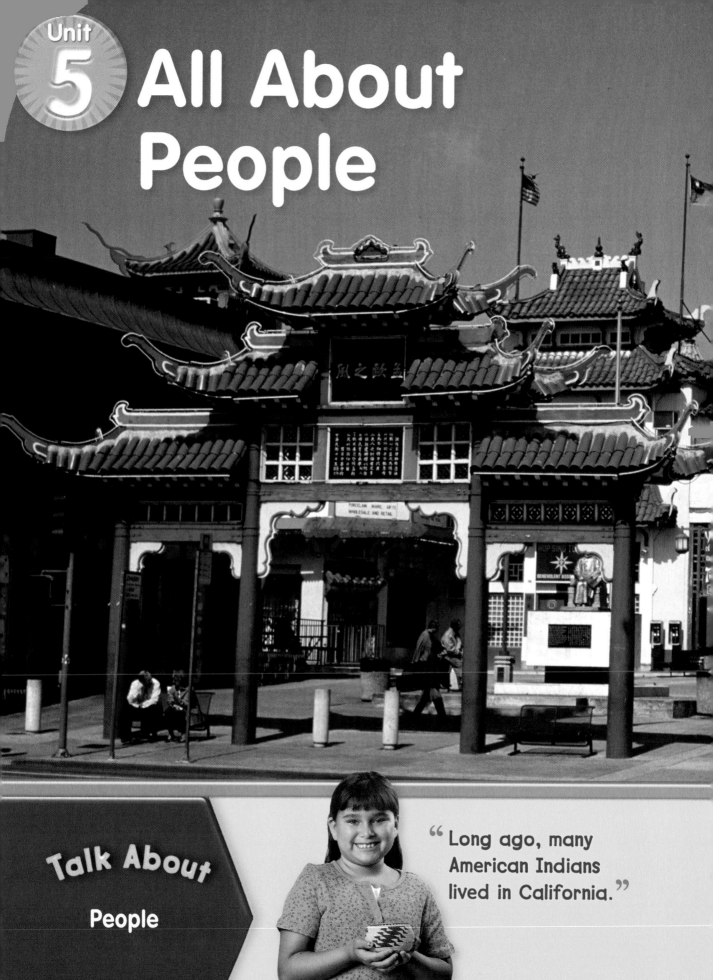

All About People

Talk About

People

"Long ago, many American Indians lived in California."

聯 合 銀 行

951

"People come from all over the world to live in the United States of America."

"We share our culture in many ways."

209

Vocabulary

culture   A group's way of life.

(page 220)

tradition   A special way of doing something that is passed on from parents to children.

(page 222)

history The story of what happened in the past. (page 228)

immigrant A person from another part of the world who has come to live in this country. (page 236)

custom A group's way of doing something. (page 251)

GO ONLINE

INTERNET RESOURCES
Go to **www.harcourtschool.com/hss** to view Internet resources for this unit.

Unit 5

Reading Social Studies

(Focus Skill) Compare and Contrast

As you read, compare and contrast things.

● You compare two things by thinking about how they are the same.

● You contrast two things by thinking about how they are different.

Practice the Skill

Read the paragraph.

Compare Mira and Rosa are best friends. Mira's family is from Poland. She speaks Polish and
Contrast English. Rosa's family is from Mexico. She speaks Spanish and English. Mira and Rosa both like to play basketball. They have different favorite foods. Mira likes a Polish soup called chlodnik. Rosa likes tortillas, a Mexican bread.

212

Mira

family is from Poland

_____

_____

Similar

They are best friends.

_____

_____

_____

Rosa

family is from Mexico

_____

_____

This chart shows how Mira and Rosa are the same and different. What can you add? Copy the chart and fill it in.

Apply as You Read

As you read, look for ways to compare and contrast different kinds of people.

Study Skills

Anticipation Guide

Sometimes your ideas about something may not be right. An anticipation guide helps you think about ideas before you read. After you read, you can use the anticipation guide to see if you were right.

Practice the Skill

The anticipation guide on the next page shows ideas about things in this unit. Read the sentences, and talk about them with another person. Then copy the anticipation guide.

- Circle **T** if you think a sentence is true.

- Circle **F** if you think a sentence is false.

214

Anticipation Guide

T	F	1. All people have the same celebrations.
T	F	2. Families who come to the United States bring their cultures with them.
T	F	3. American Indians came to the United States from another country.
T	F	4. You can learn about a culture by reading folktales.
T	F	5. People can show their culture in the way they dress.

Apply as You Read

Look back at the anticipation guide as you read this unit. Find out if your ideas were right. Talk about how your ideas changed after you read the unit.

What a Wonderful World

by George David Weiss and Bob Thiele

illustrated by Ashley Bryan

I see trees of green,

red roses too,

I see them bloom

for me and you,

and I think to myself,

"What a wonderful world!"

216

I see skies of blue
and clouds of white,
the bright, blessed day,
the dark, sacred night,
and I think to myself,
"What a wonderful world!"

217

The colors of the rainbow, so pretty in the sky
are also on the faces of people going by.
I see friends shaking hands, saying, "How do you do?"
They're really saying, "I love you."

I hear babies cry, I watch them grow.

They'll learn much more than I'll ever know,

and I think to myself,

"What a wonderful world!"

Yes, I think to myself,

"What a wonderful world!"

Response Corner

❶ What is this song telling us about the world?

❷ **Make It Relevant** What do you think is wonderful about the world?

219

Lesson

What to Know

Who belongs to a community?

- ✓ People in the same community have different cultures.

- ✓ Different people in a community share many things.

Vocabulary

culture

tradition

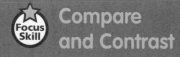

Focus Skill Compare and Contrast

California Standards
HSS 1.5, 1.5.1

People Together

Ben and his family have just moved to a new city. Ben likes learning about the different cultures in his new community. A **culture** is a group's way of life.

Ben has made a lot of friends at his new school. The children in his class come from different cultures, too.

Many things such as food, clothing, and dance are part of a group's culture. Ben has learned that different cultures make his community an interesting place to live in.

food

clothing

dance

People in a community also share many things. They respect their community and follow its traditions. A **tradition** is a special way of doing something that is passed on from parents to children.

People of different cultures live and work together in their community. Learning about how we are different and sharing traditions help us get along.

Croatian Extravaganza!

Summary A community is made up of people of different cultures who share many of their traditions.

Review

1. Who belongs to a community?

2. **Vocabulary** What is a **tradition**?

3. **Activity** Draw a picture about your culture.

4. **Compare and Contrast** Look at the children on this page. How is their clothing like yours? How is it different?

Points of View

The Sidewalk Reporter asks:
"What do you like about having many cultures in your community?"

David

"I can taste foods from around the world in the restaurants in my community."

Mr. Fernandez

"We like learning about other cultures at festivals in our community."

View from the Past

Robert C. Weaver: Many Cultures

The United States made a law saying that people of every culture have the right to live in any community. Robert C. Weaver had the job of making sure people followed this new law.

224

Mr. Peters

"I am learning some French words from the woman who owns the French bakery in my neighborhood."

Mrs. Martinez

"Artists from different cultures make murals for people in the community to enjoy."

Kelsey

"I love watching street performers play their special kinds of music!"

ANALYSIS SKILL It's Your Turn

- What cultures do you have in your community?
- How do different cultures make your community interesting?

America's First People

The first people to live in North America are called American Indians. There were many different groups, and each group had its own culture.

What to Know
How have American Indians affected our culture?

✓ American Indians were the first people to live in North America.

✓ Settlers learned many things from American Indian cultures.

Vocabulary
history
language

Focus Skill
Compare and Contrast

California Standards
HSS 1.5, 1.5.2

Nez Perce

Pomo

Mandan

Hopi

This map shows where some American Indian groups lived long ago. The place where each group lived affected its culture. Today, many American Indians still live in parts of the United States.

ANALYSIS SKILL Which American Indian group shown on this map lived where California is today?

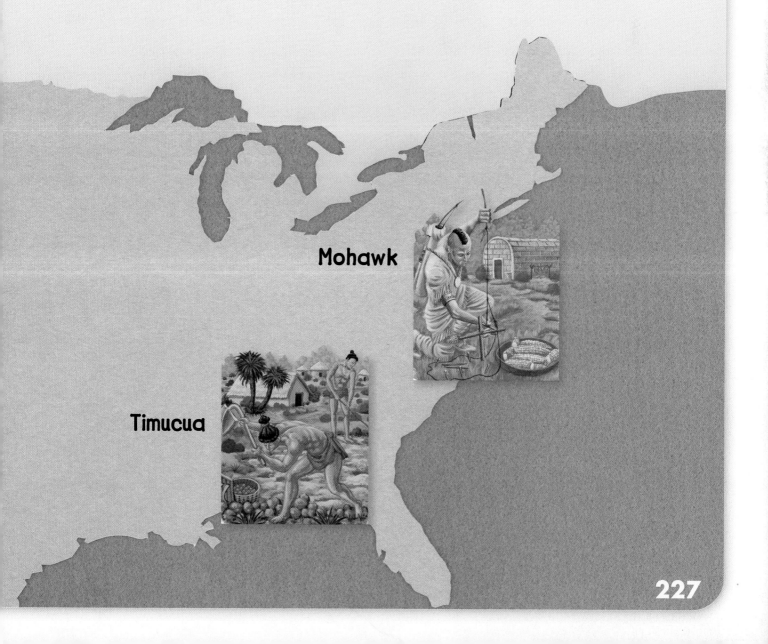

Mohawk

Timucua

These children are listening to an American Indian storyteller. He shares the history of his people. **History** is the story of what happened in the past. Some stories in history are myths. A myth is a story that tells why something in nature is the way it is.

Each American Indian group had its own **language**, or way of speaking. American Indians used language to pass down stories about their culture and traditions. We know a lot about their history through these stories that many American Indians still tell today.

⚡**Fast Fact**

All over the United States, there are places with names that come from American Indian languages. In California, the name of the city of Pasadena is an American Indian word that means "valley."

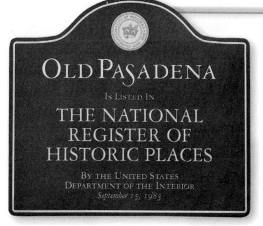

OLD PASADENA
IS LISTED IN
THE NATIONAL
REGISTER OF
HISTORIC PLACES
BY THE UNITED STATES
DEPARTMENT OF THE INTERIOR
September 15, 1983

Early settlers who came to our country learned a lot from the American Indians. The Indians told them about the land's plants and animals. They showed the settlers how to grow and cook new foods and how to make things they needed.

ANALYSIS SKILL What does this map show you about each of the American Indian groups shown?

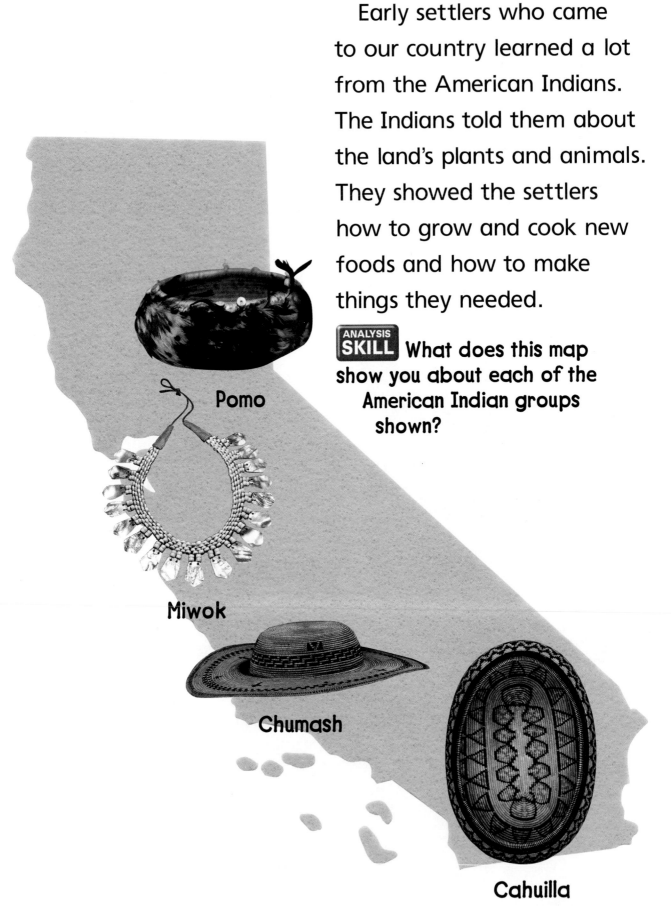

Pomo

Miwok

Chumash

Cahuilla

American Indians have a long history in California. More than 100 groups live in California today. They still honor the traditions of their cultures.

Hupa Indian basket makers

Summary American Indians helped our country grow. They shared their cultures and traditions with early settlers.

Review

1. How have American Indians affected our culture?

2. **Vocabulary** How does your family remember its **history**?

3. **Write** Write a few sentences that tell what you have learned about American Indian cultures.

4. **Compare and Contrast** Look at the American Indian crafts on page 230. How are they like things that you use?

231

Follow a Flowchart

❱ Why It Matters

A **flowchart** shows the steps needed to make or do something.

❱ What You Need to Know

The title tells what the flowchart is about. Each sentence tells about a step. Arrows show the order of the steps.

❱ Practice the Skill

1. What does this flowchart show?

2. What did the Chumash do first?

3. What did they do after they added water to the acorn powder?

The Chumash Indians ate acorn soup with every meal.

How the Chumash Indians Made Acorn Soup

1 Take the shells off the acorns.

2 Crush the acorns into a powder.

3 Add water to the acorn powder.

4 Put hot stones into the soup to cook it.

❯ Apply What You Learned

Make It Relevant   Think about something you know how to do, such as brushing your teeth. Make a flowchart that tells others how to do it.

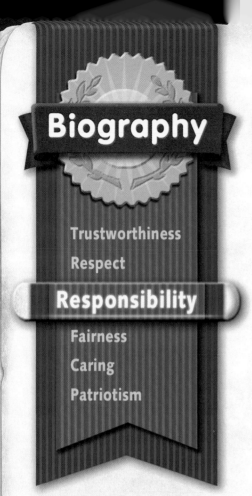

Trustworthiness

Respect

Responsibility

Fairness

Caring

Patriotism

Why Character Counts

❓ How did Sacagawea show responsibility?

Sacagawea

Sacagawea was an American Indian woman of the Shoshone tribe. As a young woman, Sacagawea met two explorers named Captain Meriwether Lewis and Captain William Clark. This meeting changed her life.

Lewis and Clark wanted to explore the western part of North America. They needed help from a person who knew the land. They asked Sacagawea to be their guide. She agreed to go with them, taking her baby son along.

Sacagawea helped Lewis and Clark explore North America.

234

Sacagawea helped Lewis and Clark speak to American Indians and learn about the land.

Sacagawea is honored with her picture on a coin.

Bio Brief

ca. 1786   ca. 1812

Important Dates

about 1804 Marries Toussaint Charbonneau

February 1805 Gives birth to a son

May 1805 Joins explorers Lewis and Clark as their guide

1809 Moves to St. Louis with her family

Sacagawea helped the American Indians they met not to be afraid of the strangers. She also got her own tribe to give the explorers horses and food. When Lewis and Clark's important papers fell into the water, Sacagawea saved them. Her responsible acts helped the explorers in many ways.

Interactive Multimedia Biographies
Visit MULTIMEDIA BIOGRAPHIES
at **www.harcourtschool.com/hss**

What to Know
How have immigrants added to our culture?

✔ Immigrants from around the world bring their cultures to the United States.

✔ People in our country are free to keep their own cultures.

Vocabulary
immigrant
world

Compare and Contrast

California Standards
HSS 1.5, 1.5.2

People Find New Homes

Anahat, Kwame, Juan, and Yana are making a scrapbook about their families. They are all immigrants to California. An **immigrant** is a person from another part of the world who has come to live in this country. The **world** is all the people and places on Earth.

Anahat is from India.

Kwame is from Ghana.

Juan is from El Salvador.

Yana is from Russia.

237

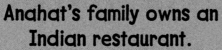

Families who come to the United States bring their cultures with them. They share their cultures and traditions with others. Many kinds of food, clothing, and recreation have been brought to this country by immigrants.

Anahat's family owns an Indian restaurant.

Kwame's family sells African art.

Yana's mother teaches ballet, which she learned in Russia.

Juan's grandmother sells cloth that she learned to make in El Salvador.

Cultural Heritage

German Immigrants

Long ago, many Americans stayed at home to rest on the weekends. German immigrants liked to do things for fun on the weekends. They went out to have picnics, listened to music, and played sports. Soon other people began to do the same. Now many Americans enjoy weekend recreation.

People have come to the United States from other places for many years. Some immigrants crossed the ocean from countries such as China, Ireland, and Italy. Others came by land from Canada and Mexico.

Angel Island, California

Russian passport

People are still coming to the United States today. When people move here, they can keep their cultures and traditions. They can share in American culture, too.

Summary Immigrants move to the United States from all over the world. The cultures they bring help our country change and grow.

Review

① 💡 How have immigrants added to our culture?

② **Vocabulary** What is the **world**?

③ ✏️ **Activity** What countries did people in your family live in before they came to the United States? Mark the places on a globe or map.

④ ⭐ **Compare and Contrast** How are Anahat, Kwame, Juan, and Yana like you? How are they different?

241

Follow a Route

❯ Why It Matters

A **route** on a map shows how to get from one place to another.

❯ What You Need to Know

On this map of California, the red line shows a route from the city of San Francisco to the city of Blythe. Imagine that you and your family are immigrants. You have just crossed the ocean to San Francisco. Now you will go to your new home in Blythe by following the route on the map.

❯ Practice the Skill

❶ Look at the map. Where does the route start and end?

❷ What river will you see at the beginning of your trip?

❸ In which direction will you go after passing Los Angeles?

❹ What other places are near the route?

242

San Francisco to Blythe

Map Legend

- → Route
- ～ River
- ● City
- National Park
- Sea

San Francisco

San Joaquin River

Los Angeles

Joshua Tree National Park

Salton Sea

Blythe

N W E S

❱ Apply What You Learned

ANALYSIS SKILL **Make It Relevant** Make a map of your school. Show the route you take from your classroom to the playground.

 Practice your map and globe skills with the **GeoSkills CD-ROM.**

4

Expressing Culture

 What to Know
What can folktales tell you about cultures?

✔ People share their cultures through stories.

✔ Some folktales from different cultures are the same story told in different ways.

Vocabulary
folktale
religion

Focus Skill Compare and Contrast

 California Standards
HSS 1.5, 1.5.3

Every culture has folktales. A **folktale** is a story passed from person to person. Most folktales were told for many, many years before they were written down on paper.

When Hare woke up, he saw that

Tortoise, slow and steady, had

You can learn about a culture by reading and listening to folktales. Words, pictures, dance, and other arts are all used to tell these stories.

he had been wrong.

won the race.

Mexican puppets

Hawaiian dancers

Vietnamese story cloth

Folktales can show many things about a culture. They can tell about its people and the places where they live. Folktales can also tell about a culture's traditions and special ways of doing things.

Folktales can tell about nature.

Folktales can show traditions.

THE NAME OF THE TREE

A BANTU FOLKTALE RETOLD BY Celia Barker Lottridge
ILLUSTRATED BY Ian Wallace

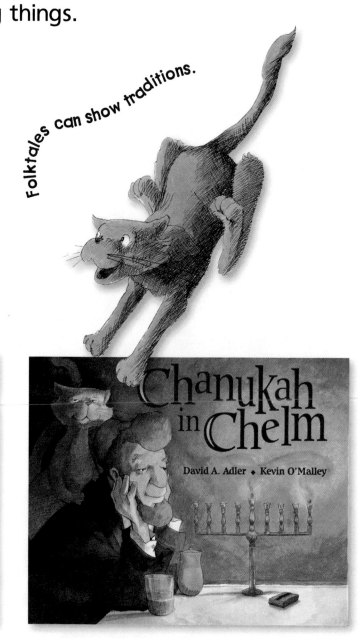

Chanukah in Chelm

David A. Adler ◆ Kevin O'Malley

Folktales can teach lessons and help you learn what people believe. Folktales can also show that cultures have different religions. A **religion** is a belief in a god or gods.

Folktales can teach lessons.

One Grain of Rice
Demi
A MATHEMATICAL FOLKTALE

Folktales can tell about beliefs.

How Night Came from The Sea
A STORY FROM BRAZIL
Retold by MARY-JOAN GERSON • Pictures by CARLA GOLEMBE

Some stories can be found in almost every culture. These folktales are the same story told in different ways and in different languages.

"Come!" he commanded. "You must try this rose-red slipper."

The servant girls gawked openmouthed as the Pharaoh kneeled before Rhodopis. He slipped the tiny shoe on her foot with ease. Then Rhodopis pulled its mate from the folds of her tunic.

"Behold!" cried Amasis. "In all this land there is none so fit to be queen!"

"But Rhodopis is a slave!" protested one of the servant girls.

Kipa sniffed. "She is not even Egyptian."

"She is the most Egyptian of all," the Pharaoh declared. "For her eyes are as green as the Nile, her hair as feathery as papyrus, and her skin the pink of a lotus flower."

The Pharaoh led Rhodopis to the royal barge, and with every step, her rose-red slippers winked and sparkled in the sun.

"Then she must deserve me as her husband," said the magistrate, "for this lucky shoe has led me to her."

"Another of Pigling's magic tricks!" hissed Omoni, pulling Peony to the palanquin. "My daughter will give you TWO shoes! That is twice as lucky!"

The magistrate looked at Omoni as if she had lost her wits; then he turned to Pear

Blossom and said, "I've luck enough if she who wears this one becomes my bride."

Pear Blossom smiled, too shy to speak, and slipped the sandal on her foot.

Omoni stood staring, stiff as a clay statue, but Peony ran straight to the rice fields to find the magic ox. All she saw was a glimpse of its hooves as it galloped away.

THE EGYPTIAN CINDERELLA

by Shirley Climo • illustrated by Ruth Heller

THE KOREAN CINDERELLA

by Shirley Climo
Illustrated by Ruth Heller

Summary People share their cultures through folktales. Folktales can tell about the traditions and beliefs of a culture.

Review

1. What can folktales tell you about cultures?

2. **Vocabulary** What is a **religion**?

3. **Activity** Act out a folktale that tells about a culture that is different from your own.

4. **(Focus Skill) Compare and Contrast** Read or listen to two Cinderella stories from different cultures. How are the two stories the same and how are they different?

What to Know
How do people show their cultures?

✔ People in different cultures have special ways of doing things.

✔ Celebrations help people share their cultures.

Vocabulary
celebration
custom

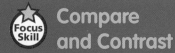 **Focus Skill** **Compare and Contrast**

California Standards
HSS 1.5, 1.5.3

Sharing Cultures

In Li's culture, the celebration of Chinese New Year lasts for 15 days. A **celebration** is a time to be happy about something special.

Each day of Chinese New Year has a different **custom**, or way of doing something. It is a custom to celebrate the last night of Chinese New Year with a Lantern Festival.

Li did not grow up in China. He is learning about his Chinese culture from the traditions, celebrations, and customs of his family and his community.

Anita's family is from Mexico. Every year on May 5, they celebrate Cinco de Mayo. Cinco de Mayo is a celebration to honor Mexico.

There are many different celebrations in our country. Each culture is proud of its customs and traditions. Sharing special celebrations helps us learn about each other.

Summary People celebrate special times. We share our culture's customs and traditions when we celebrate with others.

Review

1 How do people show their cultures?

2 **Vocabulary** What is one **celebration** that you share with your family?

3 **Activity** Make a collage about cultures. Show different customs, traditions, and celebrations.

4 **Compare and Contrast** How are Chinese New Year and American New Year celebrations the same? How are they different?

How Beetles Became Beautiful

a folktale from Brazil
illustrated by Christopher Corr

Long ago, in the country of Brazil, a brown beetle was crawling toward the Amazon River. Suddenly, a paca ran past her.

"Out of my way, Beetle!" said the plain brown and white rodent. "You are much too slow."

A bright green and yellow parrot had been watching from a tree branch above. "Paca," he called. "What is the problem?"

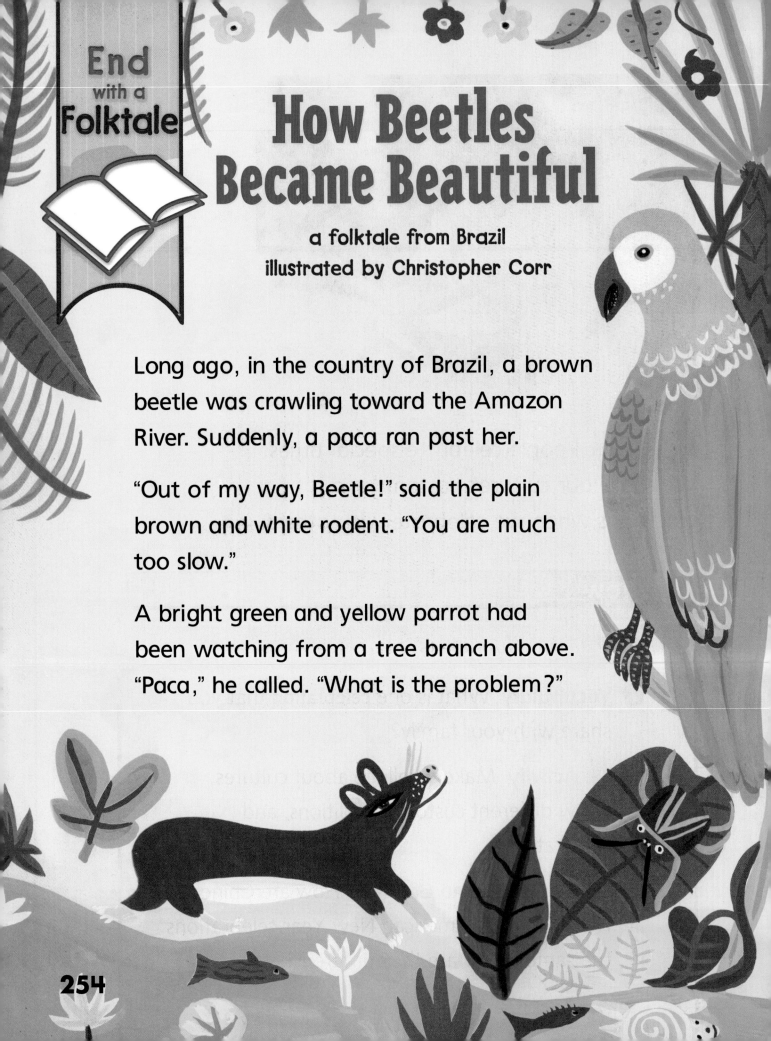

"Beetle is in my way," Paca said.

"I'm sorry," said Beetle. "I am on my way to the river."

"Ha!" said Paca. "You are so slow, you will never get there. If you were fast, like me, you would be there in no time at all."

Parrot did not like Paca's bragging. "Let's have a race," he said. "The first one to the river will earn a beautiful new coat. Now, get ready . . . get set . . . go!"

Paca and Beetle began their race as Parrot flew to the river. Paca ran far ahead of Beetle until he could no longer see her.

"Beetle will never be able to catch up with me," thought Paca. Soon Paca finished the race. "Here I am, Parrot!" he said. "I want my new coat now."

"Look beside you," said Parrot.

Paca looked down and saw Beetle sitting by the river. "How did you get here before me?" he said. "I can run much faster than you can!"

"I did not run," said Beetle. "I flew."

"Oh, no! I forgot Beetle had wings!" said Paca.

"Yes. You were too busy bragging to remember," said Parrot. "Now, Beetle, what colors would you like your coat to be?"

"Green and gold, please," said Beetle.

And so, to this day, beetles are beautiful. Pacas are still plain, but they are a little bit nicer.

Response Corner

❶ What does this story tell you about the country of Brazil?

❷ **Make It Relevant** Have you ever heard a story like this one?

Field Trip

International Festival of Masks

Get Ready

It's fun to visit the International Festival of Masks in Los Angeles, California! Masks are part of many traditions around the world. The festival's activities help people share their cultures.

Locate It
California

Los Angeles

What to See

People share their culture with music, dance, food, and storytelling.

At the festival, you can learn how to make masks and other kinds of crafts.

People show off their masks and costumes in the festival's Parade of Masks.

A Virtual Tour

GO ONLINE Visit VIRTUAL TOURS at www.harcourtschool.com/hss

Review

💡 **People** Although Americans may come from different backgrounds, they share some beliefs.

⭐ Focus Skill **Compare and Contrast**

Copy and fill in the chart to compare and contrast American Indians and immigrants.

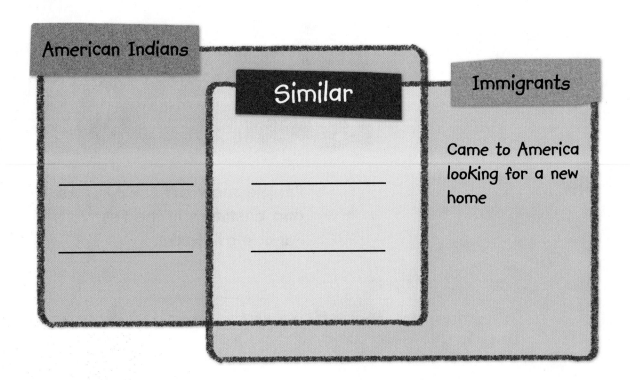

American Indians

Similar

Immigrants

Came to America looking for a new home

Use Vocabulary

Give another example to explain each word.

	Words	Examples	
❶	culture (p. 220)	American Indians' way of life	
❷	tradition (p. 222)	opening birthday presents before breakfast	
❸	history (p. 228)	Americans fought a war for freedom	
❹	immigrant (p. 236)	a person who moves to America from Germany	
❺	custom (p. 251)	Chinese dragon dance	

Recall Facts

❻ What is a special way of doing something that is passed down from parents to children?

❼ Who were the first people in North America?

❽ Where do immigrants come from?

❾ What is a folktale?

    A a story passed from person to person

    B a time to be happy about something

    C a belief in a god or gods

    D a group's way of speaking

❿ Which culture celebrates the New Year for 15 days?

    A German

    B Chinese

    C Mexican

    D American

Think Critically

⑪ **ANALYSIS SKILL** How are immigrants today like the first settlers? How are they different?

⑫ **Make It Relevant** How does your family celebrate your culture?

Apply Map and Globe Skills

⑬ Where does the route start?

⑭ What cities does the route go through before it gets to San Jose?

⑮ What large bay does the route pass?

⑯ In which direction do you travel to get from Eureka to San Jose?

Eureka to San Jose

Eureka
Redding
Santa Rosa
San Francisco
San Francisco Bay
San Jose
Sacramento
Monterey
Fresno
Bakersfield
Lompoc
Barstow
Los Angeles
San Diego
PACIFIC OCEAN

North
West — East
South

Map Legend
— Route
• City
★ Capital
∿ River

Apply Chart and Graph Skills

How to Make a Chinese Lantern

1. Fold a piece of paper in half.

2. Make small cuts along the fold.

3. Unfold the paper. Paste the short edges together.

4. Paste a strip of paper across one end to make a handle.

17. How many steps does it take to make a Chinese lantern?

18. What is the first step?

19. What do you do after you make the cuts in the paper?

20. What is the last step?

Activities

Show What You Know

Read More

Winter Celebrations by Ellen Catala

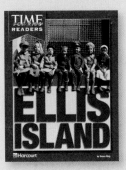

Ellis Island by Susan Ring

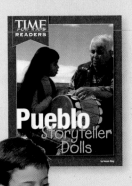

Pueblo Storyteller Dolls by Susan Ring

Unit Writing Activity

Compare Cultures Think about your culture and another culture.

Write a Paragraph Write a paragraph about how your culture is the same as and different from the other culture.

Unit Project

Culture Fair Plan a culture fair.

- Find out about a culture in your community.
- Make a booth with activities and displays.
- Hold the fair.

GO ONLINE Visit ACTIVITIES at www.harcourtschool.com/hss

The Marketplace

 Start with the Standards

1.6 Students understand basic economic concepts and the role of individual choice in a free-market economy.

The Big Idea

Markets

People trade goods and services with each other. They make choices about how to spend their money.

What to Know

✔ Why are goods and services important?

✔ What kinds of jobs do people do?

✔ Why do people buy and sell?

✔ How are goods made in a factory?

Show What You Know

★ Unit 6 Test

✎ Writing: A Story

🖌 Unit Project: A Classroom Market

The Marketplace

Talk About

Markets

" You can trade money for goods and services you want to buy. "

PLAZA
CUSTOMER
PARKING
YELLOW SECTION
2HR LIMIT
9AM-6PM
MON.-SAT.
WHITE SECTION
ALL DAY
OJAI CERTIFIED
FARMERS MARKET
SUNDAYS

STRAWBERRIES

" People do many kinds of
jobs to earn money. "

" Many of the goods that you
buy are made in factories. "

265

Vocabulary

goods Things that people make or grow to sell.

(page 276)

services Kinds of work people do for others for money.

(page 278)

trade To give one thing to get another thing.

(page 294)

factory A building in which people use machines to make goods. (page 300)

market A place where people buy and sell goods.

(page 292)

INTERNET RESOURCES

Go to **www.harcourtschool.com/hss** to view Internet resources for this unit.

Unit 6

Reading Social Studies
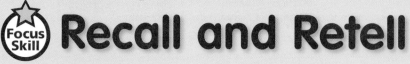
Focus Skill Recall and Retell

As you read, stop to recall and retell information.

● To recall is to remember.

● To retell is to tell about something in your own words.

Practice the Skill

Read the paragraphs.

Recall

Mr. Okada goes to work every morning and is gone all day. He put this ad in his city's newspaper.

WANTED: Honest, hard-working person to help with work around the house. Must be able to work during the day. Must also love dogs.

268

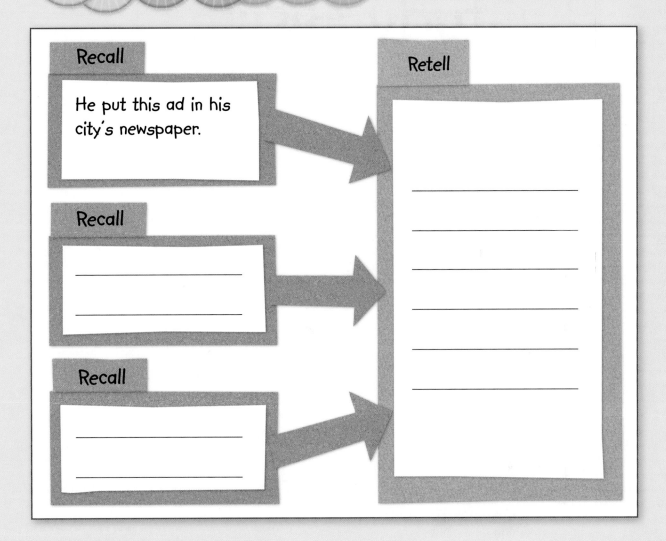

Recall

He put this ad in his city's newspaper.

Recall

Recall

Retell

Use this chart to write details you recall from what you just read. Then retell what you read in your own words. Copy the chart and fill it in.

Apply as You Read

As you read, stop to recall and retell what you have read.

Study Skills

Connect Ideas

A flowchart shows the steps it takes to make something happen. You can use a flowchart to learn about the steps it takes to make, sell, and buy things.

Practice the Skill

The flowchart on the next page shows the steps Beth and Cary follow to make and sell picture frames.

- The boxes show what happens in each step.

- The arrows show you the order in which these things happen.

Beth and Cary get craft sticks, glue, and beads.	→	Beth and Cary make the frames.
Beth and Cary use the money to buy more supplies.	←	Beth and Cary sell the frames for a dollar each.

Read the paragraph Beth wrote. How does the flowchart help you understand what you read?

Cary and I wanted to make and sell picture frames. First, we got craft sticks, glue, and beads. Next, Cary and I made the frames. Then, we sold the frames to our friends for a dollar each. Last, we used the money to buy more supplies so we could make more frames.

Apply as You Read

As you read, look for things that people buy and sell. Use a flowchart to show the steps people follow to make and sell these things.

271

WORK SONG

by Gary Paulsen

illustrated by Ruth Wright Paulsen

It is keening noise and jolting sights,
and hammers flashing in the light,
and houses up and trees in sun,
and trucks on one more nighttime run.

It is fresh new food
to fill the plates,
and flat, clean sidewalks
to try to skate,
and towering buildings
that were not there,
hanging suddenly
in the air.

It is offices filled with glowing screens
and workers making steel beams,
and ice-cream cones to lick and wear,
and all the pins that hold your hair.

It's gentle arms that lift and hold,
and all the soldiers brave and bold,
and help to fit the brand-new shoes,
and hands to show you books to use.

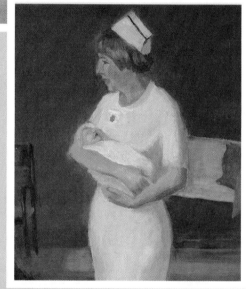

It is people here and people there,
making things for all to share;
all the things there are to be,
and nearly all there is to see.

274

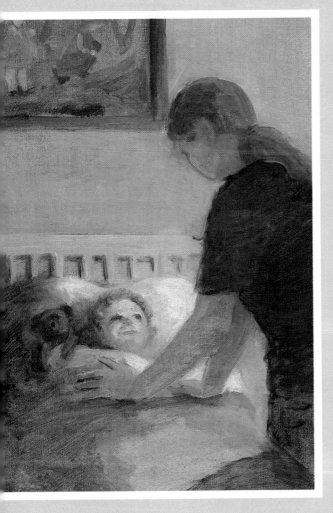

And when the day is paid and done,
and all the errands have been run,
it's mother, father in a chair,
with tired eyes and loosened hair.
Resting short but loving long,
resting for the next day's song.

Response Corner

1 What kinds of jobs does this poem tell about?

2 **Make It Relevant** Write about a job that interests you.

What to Know
Why are goods and services important?

✔ Many people earn money selling goods or services.

✔ People use money to buy what they need.

Vocabulary
goods
services
money

Recall and Retell

California Standards
HSS 1.6, 1.6.1

Goods and Services

Communities have many kinds of workers. Some workers make goods. **Goods** are things that people make or grow to sell.

Some workers sell goods. People can buy goods in stores. Communities have many kinds of stores that sell many kinds of goods.

Some workers sell services. **Services** are kinds of work people do for others for money. **Money** is what people use to pay for goods and services. You use many kinds of services in your community.

Mail carrier

Hair stylist

Services and Prices

Haircut.....................................$10

Shampoo and cut.................$12

Shampoo, cut, and style.......$16

Veterinarian

Bus driver

Summary Many people work selling goods or services. People use money to buy goods and services.

Review

1.  Why are goods and services important?

2. **Vocabulary** What is **money**?

3. ✏️ **Write** Write a sentence about a time when you used a service.

4. ⭐ (Focus Skill) **Recall and Retell** Where can people buy goods?

279

Read a Picture Graph

❯ Why It Matters

A **picture graph** uses pictures to show how many there are of something.

❯ What You Need to Know

The title tells you what a picture graph is about. The legend tells you what each picture stands for. In this graph each apple stands for one basket of apples.

Look at each row from left to right. Count to see how many baskets of each kind of apple were sold.

280

Practice the Skill

1 Look at the picture graph. Of which kind of apple were the most baskets sold?

2 Were more baskets of red apples or yellow apples sold?

3 Of which kind of apple were the fewest baskets sold?

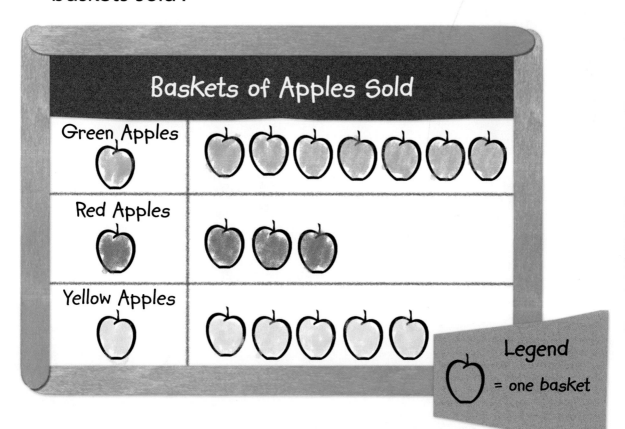

Baskets of Apples Sold

Green Apples

Red Apples

Yellow Apples

Legend
= one basket

Apply What You Learned

Make It Relevant Make a picture graph. Show which kind of apple the most children in your class like the best.

Jobs People Do

What to Know
What kinds of jobs do people do?

- ✓ People have jobs to earn money.
- ✓ A volunteer works without pay.

Vocabulary
job
business
volunteer

Recall and Retell

California Standards
HSS 1.6, 1.6.2

Mrs. Brown has a job in her community. A **job** is work that a person does to earn money. Mrs. Brown also does her job because she likes it.

Mrs. Brown owns a business. In a **business**, people sell goods or services. Mrs. Brown's business sells a service. The business helps people find jobs.

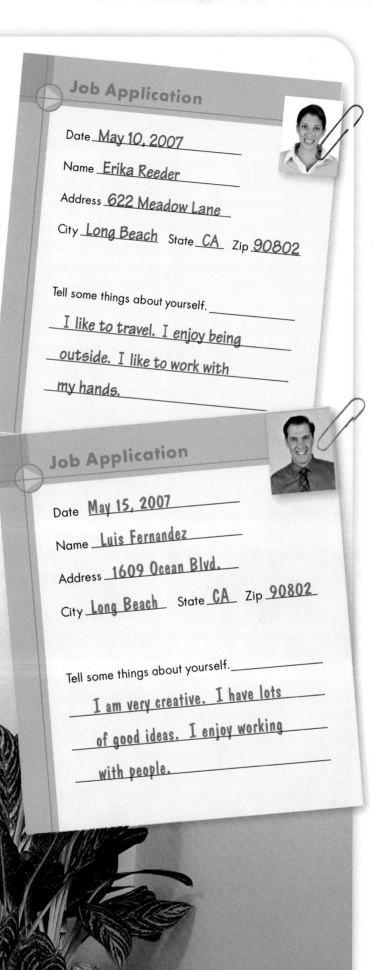

Job Application

Date May 10, 2007

Name Erika Reeder

Address 622 Meadow Lane

City Long Beach   State CA   Zip 90802

Tell some things about yourself.
I like to travel. I enjoy being outside. I like to work with my hands.

Job Application

Date May 15, 2007

Name Luis Fernandez

Address 1609 Ocean Blvd.

City Long Beach   State CA   Zip 90802

Tell some things about yourself.
I am very creative. I have lots of good ideas. I enjoy working with people.

Purchase Order

Number of Boxes Ordered	Number of Boxes Received	Cost per Box
200	200	$3.00

	Total Items	200
	Cost per Item	$3.00
	Total Cost	$600.00

Delivered by: _Erika Reeder_

There are many kinds of jobs. Many people have jobs making goods. Others have jobs taking goods where they need to go. Mrs. Brown helped Ms. Reeder find a job driving a truck to take goods to stores.

TRANSport

Many people work at jobs that help sell goods. Mrs. Brown found Mr. Fernandez a job making up ads. His ads tell people why they should buy certain goods.

California Oranges

Children in History

Addie Laird

Addie Laird was a young girl who worked in a factory. Long ago, many children had jobs in factories. They worked very hard all day, and the factory machines were not safe. When people saw this picture of Addie, they wanted to change the law. Now a child's job is to learn in school.

Some people work at taking care of their home and the people who live in it. Many people also do work for others at home. Mr. Parker gives piano lessons. Mrs. Brown takes her daughter to his house.

On Saturday, Mrs. Brown takes food to people who need it. On that day, she is a volunteer. A **volunteer** works without pay to help people.

Summary There are many kinds of jobs people can do to earn money. People can also volunteer to help others.

Review

❶ 💡 What kinds of jobs do people do?

❷ **Vocabulary** What kind of **business** would you like to own?

❸ ✏️ **Activity** Dress up to act out a job you would like to do.

❹ ⭐ **Recall and Retell** What does Mrs. Brown do to earn money?

Trustworthiness

Respect

Responsibility

Fairness

Caring

Patriotism

Why Character Counts

❖ **How did Cesar Chavez help farmworkers get fair treatment?**

Cesar Chavez

Cesar Chavez knew about the life of a farmworker. When he was a child, he and his family had to give up their farm in Arizona. They had to travel all the time to work in other people's fields. Cesar had to change schools many times. The work was hard, the hours were long, and the pay was low. Workers were treated badly. Cesar Chavez saw that this was not fair.

Cesar Chavez started a group now called the United Farm Workers of America to help workers.

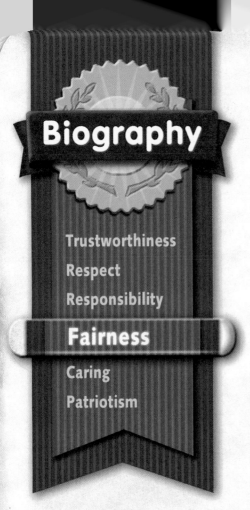

Cesar Chavez talked to people everywhere about farmworkers' rights. People trusted him because he knew what it was like to be treated unfairly as a farmworker.

In 1962, Cesar Chavez formed a union, or a group of many workers. The union held a strike. In a strike, people will not work until they are treated fairly. The farmworkers wanted better pay and health care. Cesar Chavez spent his life working to make sure people were treated fairly. ". . . [my] desire [is] to be treated fairly and to see my people treated as human beings . . ."* Cesar Chavez said.

*Cesar Chavez, from an address at the Commonwealth Club of California in San Francisco, November 9, 1984

Interactive Multimedia Biographies
Visit MULTIMEDIA BIOGRAPHIES
at **www.harcourtschool.com/hss**

Bio Brief

1927   1993

Important Dates

1962 Starts a union for farmworkers

1965 Leads the Delano Grape Strike, which lasts five years

1992 The United Farm Workers union wins better pay for workers

1994 After he dies, his work wins the Medal of Honor

Points of View

The Sidewalk Reporter asks:

"Who are some workers who have important jobs?"

Ms. Clark

"Farmers have an important job because they grow food for people to eat."

Louis

"Bus drivers have an important job. They help people get to work and to school on time."

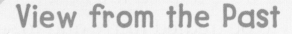

View from the Past

Rosie the Riveter

"Rosie the Riveter" was the name of a woman on a poster used in World War II. She stood for all the women who worked to help the United States in the war.

Megan

"Librarians have an important job. They help me find books I want to read."

Mr. Winslow

"People in the military have important jobs. They work to keep our country safe."

James

"Sanitation workers have an important job. They take garbage away from our homes and put it in a safe place."

We Can Do It!

ANALYSIS SKILL **It's Your Turn**

- What are some important jobs in your community?
- What job would you like to do?

What to Know
Why do people buy and sell?

✔ People trade money for goods and services.

✔ People can be buyers, sellers, or both.

Vocabulary
market
trade
save

Recall and Retell

California Standards
HSS 1.6, 1.6.1

Buyers and Sellers

Amy's community has a large outdoor market. A **market** is a place where people buy and sell goods.

Refreshments

Bonsai Booth

Amy has money to spend at the market. She is going to buy a gift for her grandmother. Amy sees that there are many choices of what to buy and where to buy it. She will think about what gift her grandmother would like best. Amy will also think about how much she has to spend.

Buyers trade with sellers to get the goods and services they want. When people **trade**, they give one thing to get another thing. Amy will trade some of her money to get a gift for her grandmother.

How Money Moves

Money moves from person to person as people buy and sell goods and services.

① Amy earns money selling lemonade.

② Amy buys a gift from Mr. Lopez.

③ Mr. Lopez pays Mr. Harris for fixing his car.

④ Mr. Harris buys lemonade.

Amy does not spend all of her money at once. She spends some of it, but she saves some, too. To **save** means to keep some money to use later. Most people put their money in a bank. A bank is a business that keeps money safe.

**" A penny saved
is a penny earned. "**

—Benjamin Franklin

from *Poor Richard's Almanack*, 1737

Summary Buyers trade money with sellers for goods and services. People save some money to use later.

Review

1. 💡 Why do people buy and sell?

2. **Vocabulary** What do people do at a **market**?

3. ✏️ **Write** Make a shopping list. Tell where you would go to buy the goods on your list.

4. ⭐(Focus Skill) **Recall and Retell** How is Amy both a seller and a buyer?

Make a Choice When Buying

▶ Why It Matters

Some things are scarce. When something is **scarce**, there is not enough of it to meet everyone's wants. **Wants** are things people would like to have. People cannot buy everything they want. They must make choices.

▶ What You Need to Know

When you make a choice, you give up some things to get other things you want. Follow these steps to make a good choice.

1. Ask yourself if you want this thing more than other things.

2. Think about what you would give up to have this thing.

3. Make your choice.

❯ Practice the Skill

① Look at the pictures. Think about which thing you would like to buy.

② Follow the steps for making a choice.

③ Tell what choice you would make and why.

❯ Apply What You Learned

ANALYSIS SKILL **Make It Relevant** Think about two things you might want. Tell how you could make a choice between the two things.

What to Know
How are goods made in a factory?

✓ Machines are used in a factory.

✓ Many people doing different jobs work together at a factory.

Vocabulary
factory

Focus Skill
Recall and Retell

California Standards
HSS 1.6, 1.6.2

Working in a Factory

We use crayons in school and at home to make pictures. Did you ever wonder how crayons are made?

Crayons are made in a factory. A **factory** is a building in which people use machines to make goods.

Manufacturing

Many people work at the crayon factory. Different workers do different jobs. Some people work in offices to take orders or to run the factory. Others work together to make the crayons, pack them, and send them to stores. Then workers at the stores sell the crayons.

Packaging

Transporting

How Crayons Are Made

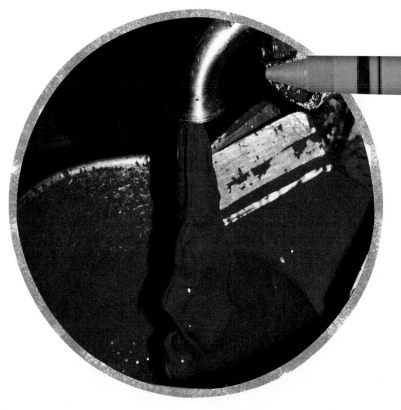

Step 1

First, the factory workers mix hot, melted wax and colorings. The wax will give the crayons their shape. The colorings will give them their colors.

Step 2

Next, workers pour the hot colored wax into molds to shape the crayons.

Step 3

Then, the molds are cooled with water so that the crayons get hard.

Step 4

Workers look at the crayons after they come out of the molds. These workers make sure that the crayons look right.

Step 5

In another part of the factory, workers use machines to make labels and paste them on the crayons.

Step 6

More workers put the crayons in boxes of different sizes. The boxes are then packed and taken to stores.

The crayons go to places around the world. Your crayons went from the factory to a store and then to your school.

Each crayon has a label that tells what color it is. These labels are in 12 different languages. Why do you think the labels are in so many languages?

azul

grün

rouge

きいろ

Summary A factory is a building in which many people use machines to make goods. People in a factory have different jobs.

Review

1. 💡 How are goods made in a factory?

2. **Vocabulary** How is a **factory** different from a market?

3. ✏️ **Activity** Draw an idea for a machine that makes something you use in the classroom. Label the parts.

4. ⭐ **Recall and Retell** How do crayons get their shape?

Use a Bar Graph

❯ Why It Matters

A **bar graph** uses bars to show how many or how much. You can use a bar graph to compare numbers or amounts of things.

❯ What You Need to Know

The title tells you what the graph shows. This graph shows how many boxes of crayons were sold at different stores.

Read each row from left to right. Each colored block stands for one box of crayons. Count the blocks to learn how many boxes were sold at each store.

▶ Practice the Skill

1 How many boxes did Mrs. Garcia's store sell?

2 Whose store sold the most boxes?

3 Who sold more boxes—Ms. Lee or Mr. Smith?

Boxes of Crayons Sold

	0	1	2	3	4	5	6	7	8

▶ Apply What You Learned

Make It Relevant Make a bar graph to show what color crayon the children in your class like the best.

ONE AFTERNOON

by Yumi Heo

Minho liked to do errands with his mother.
One afternoon, they went to
the Laundromat to drop off their clothes
and then to the beauty salon
to get his mother's hair cut.

308

At the ice cream store,
Minho got a vanilla cone.
They looked in the pet store window
at the puppies, kittens, hamsters,
and birds.

They picked up his father's shoes at the shoe repair store and got food for dinner at the supermarket.

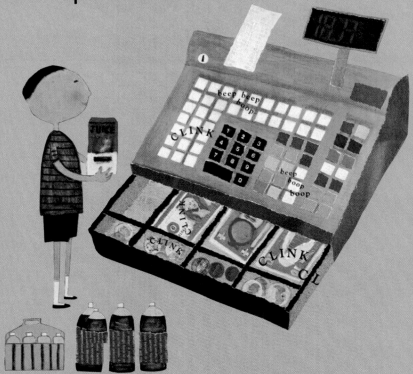

Last of all, Minho and his mother went back to the Laundromat to get the clothes they had dropped off.

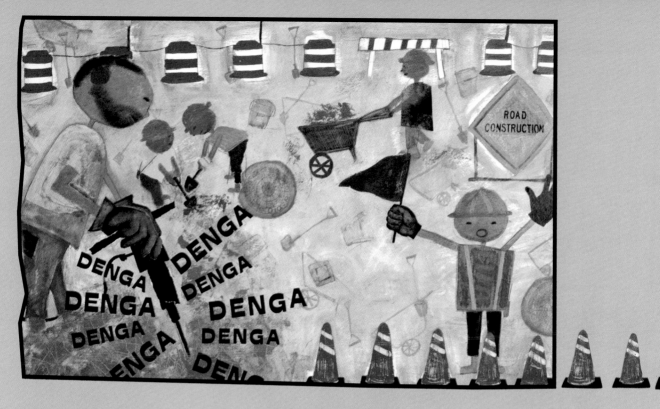

Traffic was very heavy on the street
because of the construction.
A fire engine tried to get through.
The El train was passing by above.

Near Minho's apartment,
children were playing stickball.
Minho and his mother were very
happy to get back in their quiet home.

312

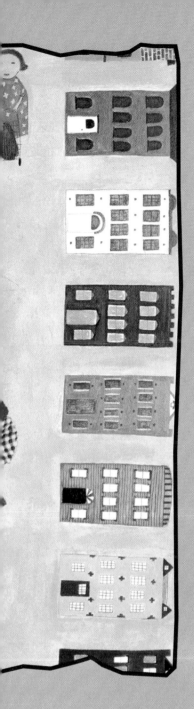

Minho was tired and fell asleep on the couch. But from the bathroom . . . PLUNK!

Response Corner

1 What services did Minho and his mother use?

2 **Make It Relevant** Write a few sentences about the kinds of goods and services your family uses in your community.

People at Work

Get Ready

In a community, people have different jobs. Many people work in offices. Others have jobs outside. Some people wear uniforms to work. People are working everywhere.

What to See

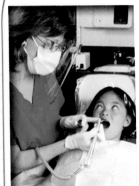

Dentist

Store clerk

Construction worker

Ballet teacher

Police officer

Taxi

Taxi driver

Architect

A Virtual Tour

GO ONLINE   Visit VIRTUAL TOURS at
www.harcourtschool.com/hss

Review

Markets People trade goods and services with each other. They make choices about how to spend their money.

Focus Skill Recall and Retell

Recall important ideas from this unit. Write them in the Recall boxes of the chart. Then retell what you remember about the ideas.

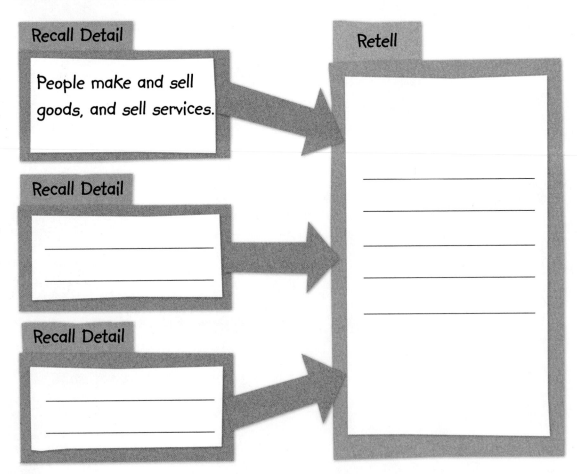

Recall Detail

People make and sell goods, and sell services.

Recall Detail

Recall Detail

Retell

Use Vocabulary

Write the word that goes with each meaning.

1. a place where people buy and sell goods

2. a building in which people use machines to make goods

3. things people make or grow to sell

4. kinds of work people do for others for money

5. to give one thing to get another

goods
(p. 276)

services
(p. 278)

market
(p. 292)

trade
(p. 294)

factory
(p. 300)

Recall Facts

6. Where do people buy goods in a community?

7. What do people use to pay for goods and services?

8. Why do people work at a job?

9. Which of these is a good?

    A haircut   **C** car wash

    B doctor   **D** bicycle

10. Which of these is a place where people put their money to keep it safe?

    A bank   **C** factory

    B market   **D** business

Think Critically

⑪ ANALYSIS SKILL Why do people save money?

⑫ **Make It Relevant** How do volunteers help people in your community?

Apply Chart and Graph Skills

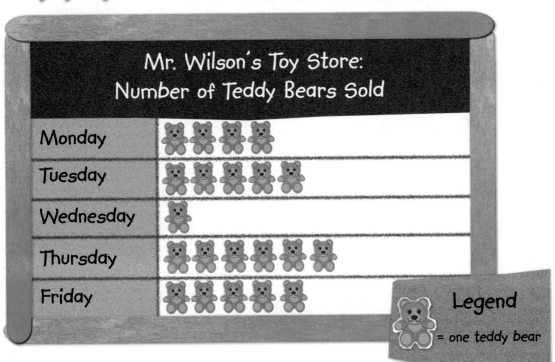

Mr. Wilson's Toy Store:
Number of Teddy Bears Sold

Monday	
Tuesday	
Wednesday	
Thursday	
Friday	

Legend
= one teddy bear

⑬ What does this graph show?

⑭ How many teddy bears were sold on Monday?

⑮ On which two days were the same number of teddy bears sold?

⑯ On which day were the fewest teddy bears sold?

Apply Chart and Graph Skills

Mr. Wheel's Car Repair Services

	0	1	2	3	4	5	6	7
Oil Change								
Car Wash								
Fix Flat Tire								
New Brakes								

⑰ What services does Mr. Wheel do for people?

⑱ What service did most people need?

⑲ How many people took their cars to Mr. Wheel for an oil change?

⑳ How many people needed new brakes?

Unit 6 Activities

Read More

Crafts by Jeri Cipriano

The Mint by Susan Ring

Many Kinds of Money by Jeri Cipriano

Unit Writing Activity

Money Think about how you use your money.

Write a Story Make up a story about someone choosing how to use his or her money.

Unit Project

Classroom Market Make a market to practice buying and selling.

- Choose what you will sell.
- Draw goods or services and money.
- Sell the goods or services so you can buy more.

GO ONLINE Visit ACTIVITIES at www.harcourtschool.com/hss

For Your Reference

Atlas

R2 World Continents

R4 World Land and Water

R6 United States States and Capitals

R8 United States Land and Water

R10 California Cities and Towns

R11 California Land and Water

Research Handbook

R12

Biographical Dictionary

R18

Picture Glossary

R20

Index

R36

ARCTIC OCEAN

NORTH AMERICA

PACIFIC OCEAN

ATLANTIC OCEAN

Equator

SOUTH AMERICA

PACIFIC OCEAN

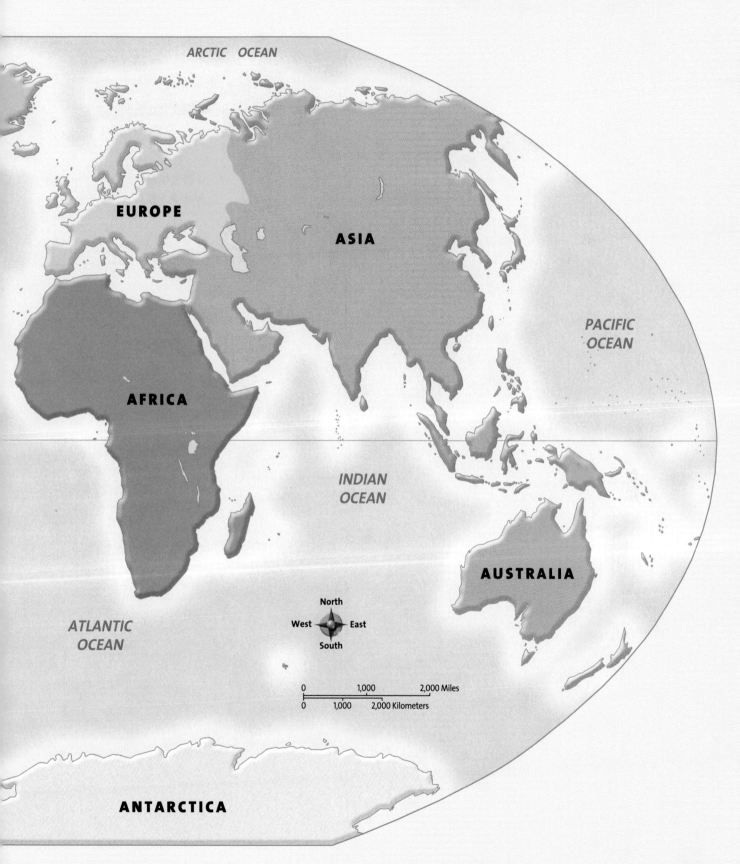

ARCTIC OCEAN

EUROPE

ASIA

AFRICA

PACIFIC
OCEAN

INDIAN
OCEAN

AUSTRALIA

ATLANTIC
OCEAN

North

West ✦ East

South

ANTARCTICA

0   1,000   2,000 Miles
0   1,000   2,000 Kilometers

R3

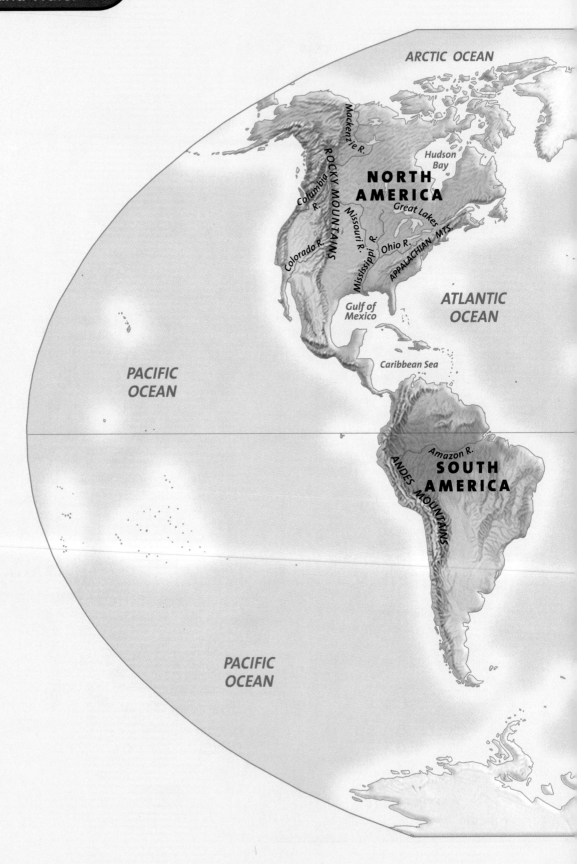

ARCTIC OCEAN

Hudson Bay

NORTH AMERICA

Mackenzie R.

ROCKY MOUNTAINS

Columbia R.

Missouri R.

Colorado R.

Mississippi R.

Ohio R.

Great Lakes

APPALACHIAN MTS.

ATLANTIC OCEAN

Gulf of Mexico

Caribbean Sea

PACIFIC OCEAN

Amazon R.

SOUTH AMERICA

ANDES MOUNTAINS

PACIFIC OCEAN

Greenland

ARCTIC OCEAN

URAL MTS.

Volga R.

EUROPE

ASIA

Sea of Okhotsk

Black Sea

Caspian Sea

GOBI (DESERT)

Mediterranean Sea

Atlas Mts.

Huang He

HIMALAYAS

PACIFIC OCEAN

Nile R.

S A H A R A

Chang Jiang

AFRICA

Ganges R.

Arabian Sea

Bay of Bengal

South China Sea

Congo River

Lake Victoria

Lake Tanganyika

Sumatra

New Guinea

INDIAN OCEAN

Madagascar

Kalahari Desert

AUSTRALIA

ATLANTIC OCEAN

GREAT VICTORIA DESERT

Darling R.

Murray R.

North

West — East

South

0   1,000   2,000 Miles

0   1,000   2,000 Kilometers

ANTARCTICA

R5

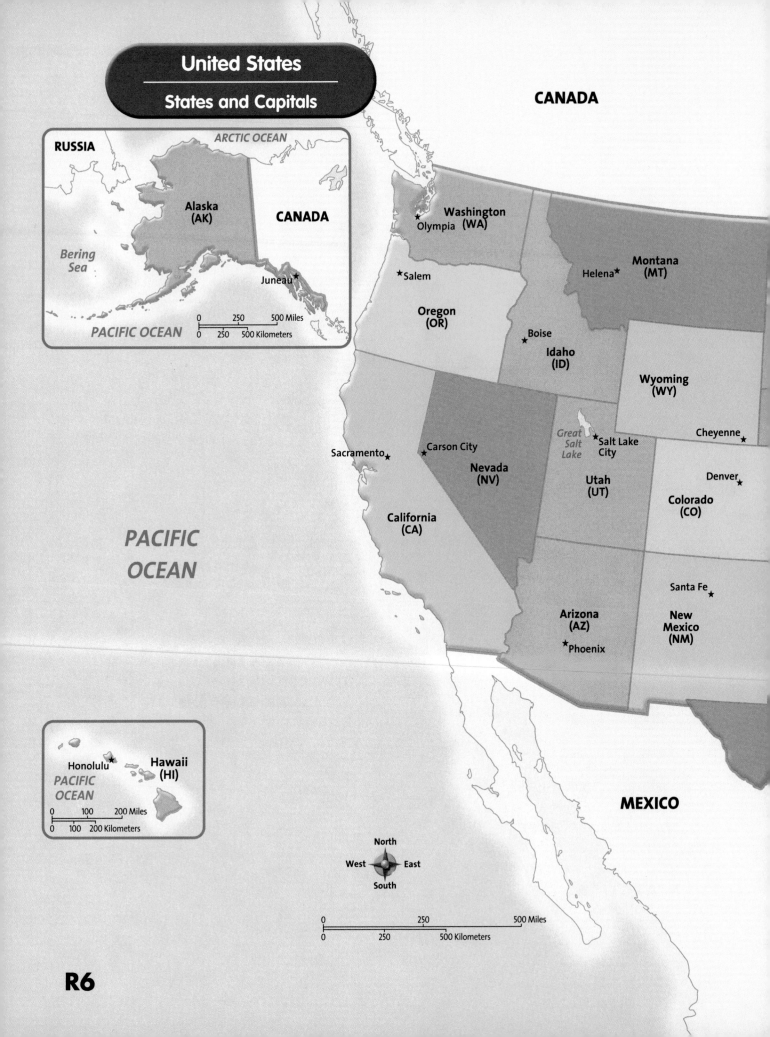

United States
States and Capitals

CANADA

RUSSIA

ARCTIC OCEAN

Alaska
(AK)

CANADA

Bering
Sea

Juneau ★

PACIFIC OCEAN

0   250   500 Miles
0   250   500 Kilometers

★ Olympia

Washington
(WA)

Montana
(MT)

Helena ★

★ Salem

Oregon
(OR)

Boise
★

Idaho
(ID)

Wyoming
(WY)

Great
Salt
Lake

★ Salt Lake
City

Cheyenne ★

Carson City
★

Sacramento ★

Nevada
(NV)

Utah
(UT)

Denver
★

Colorado
(CO)

PACIFIC

OCEAN

California
(CA)

Santa Fe
★

Arizona
(AZ)

★ Phoenix

New
Mexico
(NM)

Honolulu ★

Hawaii
(HI)

PACIFIC
OCEAN

0   100   200 Miles
0   100   200 Kilometers

MEXICO

North

West ✦ East

South

0   250   500 Miles
0   250   500 Kilometers

CANADA

North Dakota (ND)
★ Bismarck

Minnesota (MN)
St. Paul ★

Lake Superior

Lake Huron

Lake Michigan

(MI)
Lansing ★

Lake Ontario

Lake Erie

Maine (ME)
Augusta ★

Vermont (VT)
Montpelier ★

New Hampshire (NH)
★ Concord

New York (NY)
Albany ★

Boston ★
Massachusetts (MA)
★ Providence
Rhode Island (RI)

Hartford ★
Connecticut (CT)

South Dakota (SD)
★ Pierre

Wisconsin (WI)
Madison ★

Iowa (IA)
★ Des Moines

Nebraska (NE)
Lincoln ★

Illinois (IL)
Springfield ★

Indiana (IN)
Indianapolis ★

Ohio (OH)
Columbus ★

Pennsylvania (PA)
Harrisburg ★

Trenton ★
New Jersey (NJ)

Dover ★
Delaware (DE)

Annapolis
Washington D.C. ⊛
Maryland (MD)

West Virginia (WV)
Charleston ★

Virginia (VA)
Richmond ★

Topeka ★

Kansas (KS)

Missouri (MO)
Jefferson City ★

Kentucky (KY)
Frankfort ★

Oklahoma (OK)
Oklahoma City ★

Arkansas (AR)
Little Rock ★

Tennessee (TN)
Nashville ★

North Carolina (NC)
Raleigh ★

South Carolina (SC)
Columbia ★

Texas (TX)
Austin ★

Mississippi (MS)
Jackson ★

Alabama (AL)
Montgomery ★

Georgia (GA)
Atlanta ★

ATLANTIC OCEAN

Louisiana (LA)
Baton Rouge ★

Tallahassee ★

Florida (FL)

BAHAMAS

Gulf of Mexico

CUBA

R7

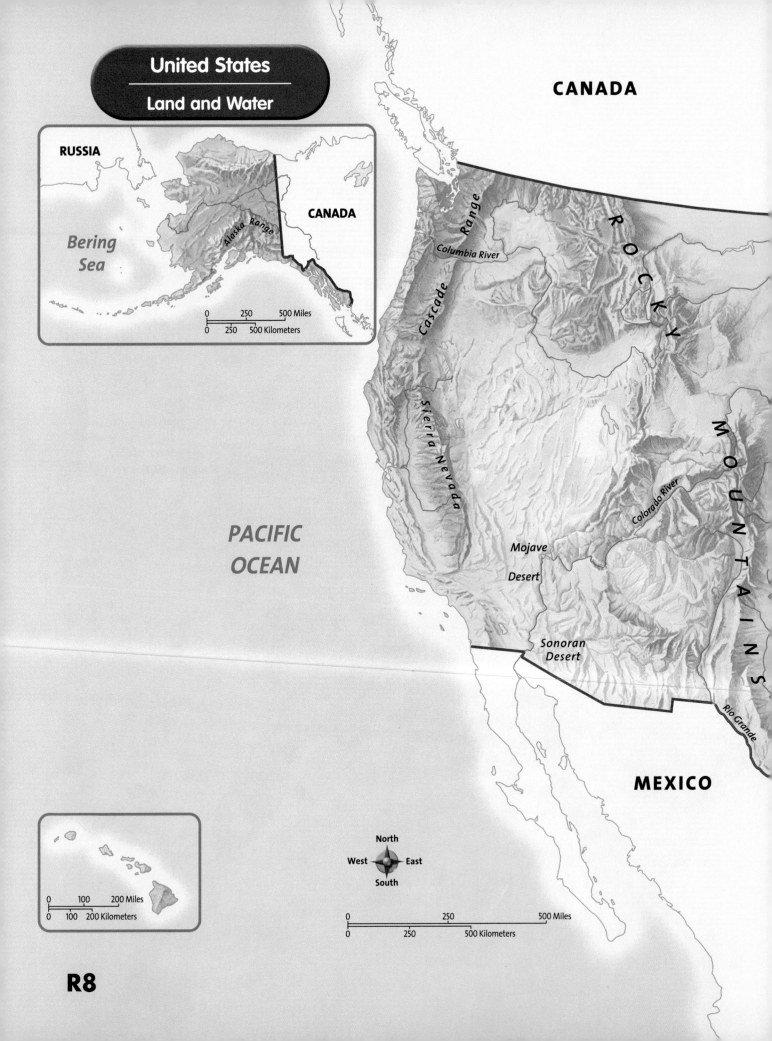

United States
Land and Water

RUSSIA

CANADA

Bering Sea

Alaska Range

| 0 | 250 | 500 Miles |
| 0 | 250 | 500 Kilometers |

CANADA

Columbia River

Cascade Range

R O C K Y

Sierra Nevada

M O U N T A I N S

Colorado River

PACIFIC OCEAN

Mojave Desert

Sonoran Desert

Rio Grande

MEXICO

| 0 | 100 | 200 Miles |
| 0 | 100 | 200 Kilometers |

North
West East
South

| 0 | 250 | 500 Miles |
| 0 | 250 | 500 Kilometers |

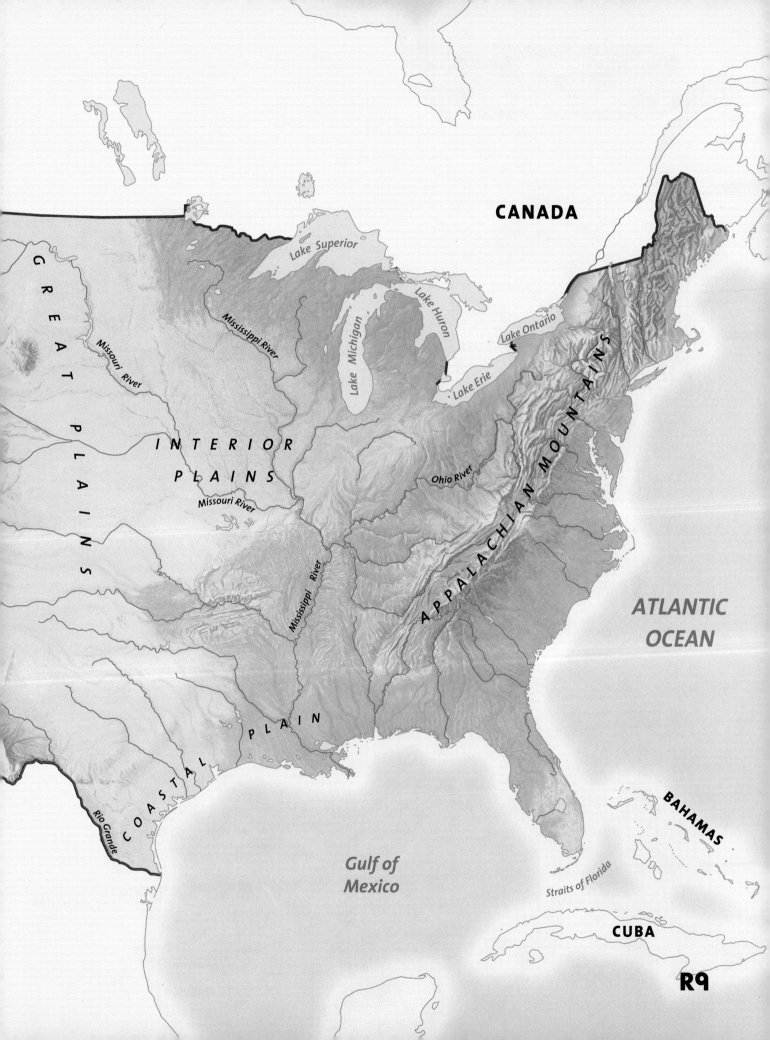

CANADA

GREAT PLAINS

Missouri River

Lake Superior

Mississippi River

Lake Michigan

Lake Huron

Lake Ontario

Lake Erie

INTERIOR PLAINS

Missouri River

Ohio River

APPALACHIAN MOUNTAINS

ATLANTIC OCEAN

Mississippi River

COASTAL PLAIN

Rio Grande

BAHAMAS

Gulf of Mexico

Straits of Florida

CUBA

California

Cities and Towns

OREGON

IDAHO

Crescent City

•Yreka

Klamath River

Goose Lake

•Alturas

River

Pit

Eureka•

Trinity River

Redding•

Shasta Lake

Susanville•

Eel River

Red Bluff•

Sacramento River

•Chico

Pyramid Lake

•Ukiah

Yuba
City•

River

Woodland•

American River

Lake Tahoe

•Placerville

★ Sacramento

Santa
Rosa•

•Napa

Stockton•

River

Stanislaus

Mono Lake

San Francisco• •Oakland

San Francisco Bay

•San Jose

•Merced

Madera•

San Joaquin River

•Hollister

•Salinas

Monterey Bay

Fresno•

Kings River

River

Monterey•

•Visalia

Tulare•

San

Salinas River

River

Kern River

•Ridgecrest

San Luis•
Obispo

Bakersfield•

•Barstow

•Santa Maria

Needles•

North
West ◆ East
South

•Lompoc

Santa
Barbara•

Santa
Clarita•

Ventura•

Pasadena•

San Bernardino•

Oxnard•

Los Angeles•

•Riverside

Torrance•

Anaheim•

•Palm Springs

Long Beach•

•Santa Ana

Blythe•

Huntington
Beach•

PACIFIC OCEAN

Salton Sea

Colorado River

Oceanside•

•Escondido

San Diego•

•El Centro

San Diego Bay

Map Legend

★ State capital
• Other city or town
— National border
— State border

NEVADA

Lake Mead

ARIZONA

MEXICO

0   75   150 Miles
0   75   150 Kilometers

R10

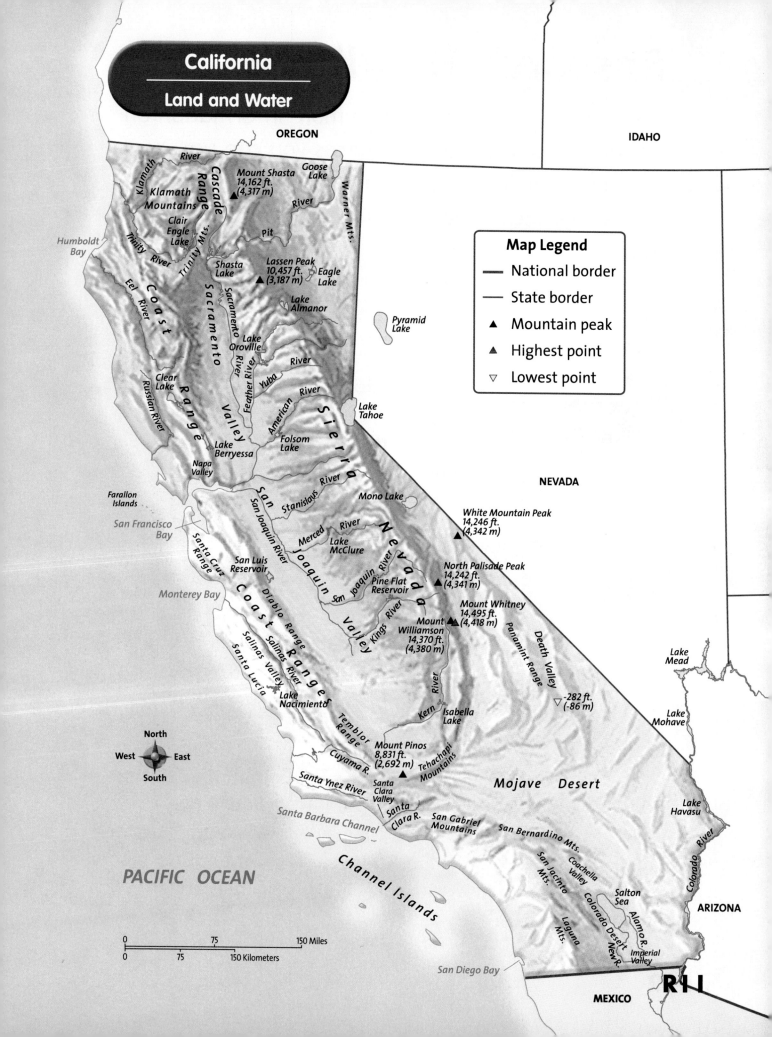

California
Land and Water

OREGON

IDAHO

Klamath River

Cascade Range

Mount Shasta
14,162 ft.
(4,317 m)

Goose Lake

Klamath Mountains

River

Clair Engle Lake

Pit

Trinity Mts.

Warner Mts.

Humboldt Bay

Trinity River

Shasta Lake

Lassen Peak
10,457 ft.
(3,187 m)

Eagle Lake

Coast Range

Eel River

Sacramento Valley

Lake Almanor

Lake Oroville

Sacramento River

River

Map Legend

— National border
— State border
▲ Mountain peak
▲ Highest point
▽ Lowest point

Clear Lake

Feather River

Yuba

River

Pyramid Lake

Russian River

American River

Sierra

Lake Berryessa

Folsom Lake

Lake Tahoe

Napa Valley

Farallon Islands

San Francisco Bay

San Joaquin River

Stanislaus River

Mono Lake

NEVADA

White Mountain Peak
14,246 ft.
(4,342 m)

Santa Cruz Range

Merced River

Lake McClure

San Joaquin River

North Palisade Peak
14,242 ft.
(4,341 m)

San Luis Reservoir

Monterey Bay

Diablo Range

San Joaquin Valley

Pine Flat Reservoir

Kings River

Mount Whitney
14,495 ft.
(4,418 m)

Mount Williamson
14,370 ft.
(4,380 m)

Coast Ranges

Salinas River

Salinas Valley

Santa Lucia

Lake Nacimiento

Kern River

Death Valley

Panamint Range

−282 ft.
(−86 m)

Lake Mead

Lake Mohave

Isabella Lake

Temblor Range

North
West — East
South

Cuyama R.

Mount Pinos
8,831 ft.
(2,692 m)

Tehachapi Mountains

Mojave Desert

Lake Havasu

Santa Ynez River

Santa Clara Valley

Santa Barbara Channel

Santa Clara R.

San Gabriel Mountains

San Bernardino Mts.

Coachella Valley

Colorado River

PACIFIC OCEAN

Channel Islands

San Jacinto Mts.

Colorado Desert

Salton Sea

Alamo R.

ARIZONA

New R.

Laguna Mts.

Imperial Valley

0   75   150 Miles
0   75   150 Kilometers

San Diego Bay

MEXICO

Research Handbook

Sometimes you need to find more information on a topic. There are many resources you can use. You can find some information in your textbook. Other sources are technology resources, print resources, and community resources.

Technology Resources
- Internet
- Computer disk
- Television or radio

Print Resources
- Atlas
- Dictionary
- Encyclopedia
- Nonfiction book
- Magazine or newspaper

Community Resources
- Teacher
- Museum curator
- Community leader
- Older citizen

Technology Resources

The main technology resources you can use are the Internet and computer disks. Television or radio can also be good sources of information.

Using the Internet

Information on the Internet is always changing. Some websites have mistakes. Be sure to use a site you can trust.

❯ Finding Information

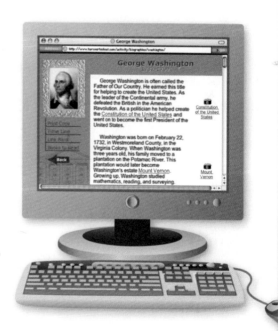

- Write down key words to look for. Make sure you spell words correctly.
- Use a mouse and a keyboard to search for information.
- With help from a teacher, parent, or older child, find the source you want to search.
- Type in your key words.
- Read carefully and take notes.
- If your computer is hooked to a printer, you can print out a paper copy.

Print Resources

Books in libraries are placed in a special order. Each book has a call number. The call number tells you where to look for the book.

Some books, such as encyclopedias, and magazines and newspapers are kept together in a separate place. Librarians can help you find what you need.

❭ Atlas

An atlas is a book of maps. Some atlases show different places at different times.

❭ Dictionary

A dictionary gives the correct spelling of words. It tells you what words mean, or their definitions. It also gives the words' pronunciations, or how to say the words aloud. Words in a dictionary are listed in alphabetical order. Guide words at the top of the pages help you find your word.

dic•tion•ar•y [dik′shən•er′ē] n., pl. dic•tion•ar•ies A reference book that lists words in alphabetical order. It gives information about the words, including what they mean and how they are pronounced.

Encyclopedia

An encyclopedia is a book or set of books that gives information about many different topics. The topics are listed in alphabetical order. An encyclopedia is a good place to start looking for information. You can also find encyclopedias on your computer.

Nonfiction Books

A nonfiction book gives facts about real people, places, and things. Nonfiction books in the library are grouped by subject. Each subject has a different call number. Look in a card file or computer catalog to find a call number. You can look for titles, authors, or subjects.

Magazines and Newspapers

Magazines and newspapers are printed by the day, week, or month. They are good sources of current information. Many libraries have a guide that lists articles by subject. Two guides are the <u>Children's Magazine Guide</u> and <u>Readers' Guide to Periodical Literature</u>.

Community Resources

Often, people in your community can tell you information you need. You can learn facts, opinions, or points of view by asking good questions. Before you talk to anyone, always ask a teacher or a parent for permission.

Listening to Find Information

❯ Before

- Think about what you need.

- Decide who to talk to.

- Make a list of useful questions.

❯ During

- Speak clearly and loudly.

- Listen carefully. You may think of other questions you want to ask.

- Be polite. Do not interrupt or argue.

  - Take notes to help you remember ideas.

  - Write down or tape-record the person's exact words for quotes. Get their permission to use the quotes.

  - Later, write a thank-you letter.

Writing to Get Information

You can also write to people in your community to gather information. You can write an e-mail or a letter. Keep these ideas in mind as you write:

- Write neatly or use a computer.
- Say who you are and why you are writing. Be clear about what you want to know.
- Carefully check your spelling and punctuation.
- If you are writing a letter, put in a self-addressed, stamped envelope for the person to send you a response.
- Thank the person.

Biographical Dictionary

The Biographical Dictionary lists many of the important people introduced in this book. Names are listed in alphabetical (ABC) order by last name. After each name are the birth and death dates. If the person is still alive, only the birth year is given. The page number tells where the main discussion of each person starts.

Adams, **John** (1735–1826) Second President of the United States. He also served two terms as America's first Vice President. p. 130

Aesop Greek storyteller. He told fables that children still enjoy today. p. 38

Bellamy, **Francis** (1855–1931) Writer of the Pledge of Allegiance. p. 110

Burns, **Julia Pfeiffer** (1868–1928) Pioneer woman of the Big Sur area of California. p. 139

Carson, **Rachel** (1907–1964) American writer. Her books encouraged many people to take better care of nature. p. 78

Chavez, **Cesar** (1927–1993) Labor leader. He united many farmworkers to demand better treatment. p. 288

Cigrand, **Bernard** (1866–1932) Teacher and dentist. He is known as the founder of Flag Day. p. 118

Coleman, **Bessie** (1892–1926) African American woman pilot. p. 182

Confucius (551 B.C.–479 B.C.) China's most famous teacher and philosopher. His personal goal was to encourage peace. p. 31

Fong, Heather (1956–) Chief of police of San Francisco, California. She is the first Asian American woman to run a big city police department. p. 37

Key, Francis Scott (1779–1843) Lawyer and poet who wrote the words of "The Star-Spangled Banner." p. 109

King, Dr. Martin Luther, Jr. (1929–1968) African American minister and leader. He worked to win civil rights for all Americans. pp. 114, 138

Marshall, James (1810–1885) First person to find gold in California, which led to the gold rush in 1849. p. 84

Parker, George S. (1867–1953) One of the founders of a company that still makes popular games today. He published his first game when he was 16 years old. p. 162

Reagan, Ronald (1911–2004) Fortieth President of the United States and former governor of California. p. 139

Sacagawea (c. 1786–1812) American Indian woman who helped Lewis and Clark explore parts of the United States. p. 234

Washington, George (1732–1799) First President of the United States. He is known as "The Father of Our Country." p. 28

Weaver, Robert C. (1907–1997) First African American to serve in the United States Cabinet. p. 224

Picture Glossary

The Picture Glossary has important words and their definitions. They are listed in alphabetical (ABC) order. The pictures help you understand the meanings of the words. The page number at the end tells where the word is first used.

B

ballot

A paper that shows all the choices in a vote. (page 26)

border

The place where a state or country ends. (page 60)

bar graph

A graph that uses bars to show how many or how much. (page 306)

business

The selling of goods or services. (page 283)

C

calendar

A chart that shows time. (page 116)

change

To become different. (page 158)

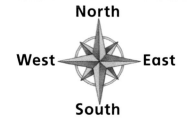

cardinal directions

The four main directions. (page 76)

citizen

A person who lives in and belongs to a community. (page 18)

celebration

A time to be happy about something special. (page 250)

city

A large community. (page 23)

colony

A land ruled by another country. (page 127)

continent

A large area of land. (page 62)

communication

The sharing of ideas and feelings. (page 188)

country

An area of land with its own people and laws. (page 60)

community

A group of people who live and work together. It is also the place where they live. (page 18)

culture

A group's way of life. (page 220)

custom
A group's way of doing something. (page 251)

Earth
Our planet. (page 62)

diagram
A picture that shows the parts of something. (page 124)

Fact The Liberty Bell cracked in 1835.

fact
Something that is true and not made up. (page 180)

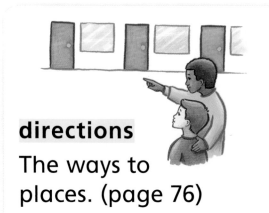

directions
The ways to places. (page 76)

factory
A building in which people use machines to make goods. (page 300)

fair
Acting in a way that is right and honest. (page 15)

flag
A piece of cloth with colors and shapes that stand for things. (page 106)

farm
A place for growing plants and raising animals. (page 72)

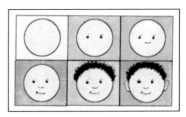

flowchart
A chart showing steps needed to make or do something. (page 232)

fiction
Stories that are made up. (page 180)

folktale
A story passed from person to person. (page 244)

freedom

The right people have to make their own choices. (page 129)

goods

Things that people make or grow to sell. (page 276)

future

The time that is to come. (page 169)

government

A group of people who lead a community. (page 24)

globe

A model of Earth. (page 62)

group

A number of people working together. (page 22)

H

hero
A person who does something brave or important to help others. (page 112)

history
The story of what happened in the past. (page 228)

I

immigrant
A person from another part of the world who has come to live in this country. (page 236)

J

job
Work that a person does to earn money. (page 282)

L

landmark
A symbol that is a place people can visit. (page 122)

language
A group's way of speaking. (page 229)

R26

M

law

A rule that people in a community must follow. (page 19)

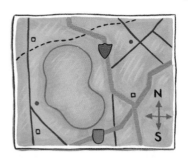

map

A picture that shows locations. (page 58)

leader

A person who is in charge of a group. (page 22)

map legend

Shows what each symbol on a map stands for. (page 68)

location

The place where something is. (page 58)

market

A place where people buy and sell goods. (page 292)

mayor

The leader of a city. (page 23)

neighborhood

A part of a town or city. (page 64)

money

What people use to pay for goods and services. (page 278)

nonfiction

Stories about real things. (page 180)

 N

national holiday

A day to honor a person or an event that is important to our country. (page 113)

 O

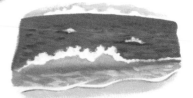

ocean

A large body of water. (page 62)

past
The time before now.
(page 166)

present
The time now.
(page 167)

picture graph
A graph that uses pictures to show how many there are of something. (page 280)

President
The leader of the United States. (page 26)

pledge
A kind of promise. (page 108)

principal
The leader of a school. (page 14)

problem

Something that is hard to solve, or fix. (page 16)

resource

Anything that people can use. (page 71)

R

recreation

What people do for fun. (page 83)

respect

To treat someone or something well. (page 30)

religion

A belief in a god or gods. (page 247)

responsibility

Something that people should do. (page 13)

right

Something people are free to do. (page 32)

save

To keep something, such as money, to use later. (page 296)

route

A way to go from one place to another. (page 242)

scarce

Not enough of something. (page 298)

rule

An instruction that tells people how to act. (page 12)

season

A time of year. (page 81)

services
Kinds of work people do for others for money. (page 278)

shelter
A home. (page 74)

settler
A person who makes a home in a new place. (page 126)

solution
An answer to a problem. (page 16)

share
To use something with others. (page 34)

sportsmanship
Playing fairly. (page 34)

R32

state

A part of a country. (page 59)

teacher

A person who leads the class. (page 12)

symbol

A picture or object that stands for something. (page 68)

technology

All of the tools we use to make our lives easier. (page 176)

table

School Lunch Times	
Class	Times
Mr. Turner	11:00 a.m.
Mrs. Rojas	11:15 a.m.
Mrs. Brown	11:30 a.m.

A chart that shows things in groups. (page 164)

time line

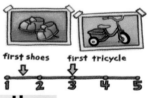

first shoes   first tricycle

1   2   3   4   5

A line that shows the order in which things have happened. (page 170)

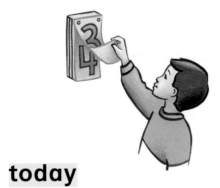

today
This day. (page 116)

trade
To give one thing to get another. (page 294)

tomorrow
The day after today. (page 116)

tradition
A special way of doing something that is passed on from parents to children. (page 222)

tool
Something a person uses to do work. (page 160)

transportation
Any way of moving people and things. (page 75)

R34

volunteer

A person who works without pay to help people. (page 287)

weather

The way the air feels outside. (page 80)

vote

A choice that gets counted. (page 26)

world

All the people and places on Earth. (page 236)

wants

Things people would like to have. (page 298)

yesterday

The day before today. (page 116)

PICTURE GLOSSARY

Index

The index tells where information about people, places, and events in this book can be found. The entries are listed in alphabetical order. Each entry tells the page or pages where you can find the topic.

A

Adams, John, 130, R18
Address, 110
Adobe, 74
Aesop, 38, R18
African Americans, 114, 138, 182–183, 224
"America" (Smith), 104–105
America, first people in, 226–231
American heroes, 112–115
American Indians, 215, 226–231
  artifacts of, 230
  culture of, 215, 226, 229
  in California, 226–227, 230, 231
  and early explorers, 234–235
  and early settlers, 230–231
  language of, 229
  storyteller, 228
  territory of, 226–227
  tribes of, 226–227, 230, 234
American River, 84
American symbols, 97–98, 100, 103, 106–109, 114, 120–123, 124–125, 128–129, 132–133
Analysis skills, 46, 58, 59, 60, 61, 63, 85, 94, 117, 126, 133, 162, 167, 171, 181, 193, 225, 227, 230, 243, 262, 291, 299

Ancestry, 195
Angel Island, California, 240
Anticipation Guide, 214–215
Apples, 169
Art, 225
Artifacts, 230
Atlantic Ocean, 126
Atlas, R2–R11, R14

B

Bald eagle, 100–101, 121
Ballot, 26, 27
Bank, 296
Bar graph, 306–307, 319
Beliefs, 247, 249, 260
Bellamy, Francis, 110–111, R18
Big Sur, 138–139
Biographies, 28–29, 78–79, 110–111, 182–183, 234–235, 288–289
Blythe, 243
Border, 60, 63
Brazil, 254–257
Bryan, Ashley, 216–219
Burns, Julia Pfeiffer, 139, R18
Business, 283, 287, 296
Butterflies, 84
Buyers, 277, 292–294, 297, 298–299

C

Cahuilla Indians, 230
Calendar, 116–117, 142

California
  animals found in, 90–91
  capital of, 24, 42
  the capitol, 24, 42–43
  cities and towns in, 19, 24, 37, 42, 52, 59, 72, 138, 139, 166, 172, 187, 202, 229, 240, R10
  counties in, 20, 74
  deserts in, 52, 82
  government of, 42–43
  landforms, 52, 55, 70, 84, 235
  maps of, 24, 42, 50, 59, 61, 90, 138, 202, 230, 243, 258, 262, R10–R11
  national parks in, 52, 90
  rivers in, 84
  state parks in, 139, 202–203
  state seal of, 42
  theme parks in, 52
  weather, 80–83
Camera, 166, 167, 193
Canada, 240
Capital, 24, R6–R7
Capitol, 105, 122, 143
Cardinal directions, 76, 95
Caring, 78–79
Carson, Rachel, 78–79, R18

Categorize, 52–53
Cause, 4–5
Celebrations, 115, 250–253
Change, 147, 151, 158, 204
  jobs and, 168–169
  technology and, 174–179
  time and, 158–163, 164–165, 166–169
Chavez, Cesar, 288–289, R18
Children in History, 123, 162, 285
"Children of Long Ago" (Little), 152–157
China, 31, 240
Chinese Lantern, How to Make a, 263
Chinese New Year, 250–251
Chlodnik, 212
Choices, 99, 129, 298
  buying, 298–299
  recreation, 83
  spending, 316
  voting, 3, 7, 24, 26–27
Chumash Indians, 230
  Acorn Soup, 233
Cigrand, Bernard, 118, R18
Cinco de Mayo, 252
Citizens, 2, 18
  character traits of, 28–29, 78–79, 110–111, 182–183, 234–235, 288–289
  honoring, 138–139
  responsibilities of, 33, 44
  rights of, 32, 33
Citizenship, 18–21, 36–37, 44, 118–119, 172–173

City, 23, 59, 243
Clark, Captain William, 234–235
Classify, 52
Clothing, 82, 185, 221, 223, 229, 238
  long ago, 146, 151
  today, 147
Coleman, Bessie, 182–183, R18
Colony, 127–128, 131
Columbia State Historic Park, 202–203
Communication, 188–189
Community, 2, 18, 21
  changes in, 166–169
  different cultures in, 220–223
  honoring their citizens, 138–139
  laws of, 3, 18–21, 36–37
  leaders in, 22–25
  long ago, 166–169
  responsibilities of citizens in, 33
Community history, 166–169
Compare, 212–213
Confucius, 31, R19
Constitution of the United States, 29, 100, 129, 133
Continent, 51, 62–63, R2–R5
Contrast, 212–213
Cote, Nancy, 134–137
Country, 50, 60, 61, 236, 237, 239, 240
  leader of, 26, 28–29
  map of, 60, 226–227
Crayon factory, 300–305
Crayons, 302–305
Cultural Heritage, 31, 74, 239

Culture, 220–223
  of American Indians, 215, 226, 229
  celebrations and, 224, 250, 250–252
  defined, 210, 220
  expressing, 244–249
  festival of, 224
  learning about, 244–249
  sharing, 209, 221–222, 230, 231, 238, 258–259
Customs, 211, 251–253

D

Dam, 71
Dance, 215, 221, 245, 259
Death Valley, 52, 82
Declaration of Independence, 100, 128–129, 132
Democracy
  direct, 26–27
  representative, 26
Deserts, 114, 70–71
  Death Valley, 52, 82
  Mojave Desert, 52
Detail, 100
Diagram, 124–125
Directions, 76
  cardinal, 76
  on maps, 76–77, 95, 126, 127, 243, 262
Diversity, 209, 212–213, 220–223, 224, 225, 226–227, 229–231, 234–235, 236–241, 246–249, 252–253, 258–259, 260
Documents, 100, 128–129, 130–133
  Bessie Coleman's pilot's license, 183

Constitution of the United States, 29, 100, 129, 133
Declaration of Independence, 100, 128–129, 132
John Adams's journal, 130

E

Eagle, 100–101, 121
Earlier generations, 184–189
   communication, 188–189
   dress, 185
   festivals, 187
   games, 187
   home tools, 190–193
   stories, 172–173
   work, 186
Earth, 62, 178, 236
East, 76, 95
Eggbeater, 190
Effect, 4
Emans, Elaine V., 56–57
England, 127–128
Europe, 126
Exchange, 294, 297
Exploration, 234–235
Explorers, 234–235

F

Fables
   <u>Lion and the Mouse, The</u> (Aesop), 38–41
Fact, 180–181
Factory, 267, 300–305
Fair, 15
Fair play, 15, 34–35
Fairness, 288–289
Fall, 81

Family
   long ago, 148, 150–151
   storytelling from, 172–173
Farm, 72
Farmers, 290
Farmworkers, 288–289
Festivals, 187, 224, 258–259
Fiction, 180–181
Flag, 98, 106–109, 118–119, 121
Flag Day, 118–119
Flowchart, 46, 232–233, 263, 270–271, 295
Folktale, 244–249
Folktales
   "How Beetles Became Beautiful" (a Folktale from Brazil), 254–257
Fong, Heather, 37, R19
Food, 72–73, 85, 212, 221, 224, 238, 259, 290
Ford, M. Lucille, 8–11
Forest, 114, 71
Fourth of July, 128
France, 103, 183
Franklin, Benjamin, 128, 142, 297
Freedom, 29, 99, 100, 103, 128–129
   of religion, 32
   of speech, 32
Free-market economy, 270–271, 276–281
friendship, 8–11
"Friendship's Rule" (Ford), 8–11
Future, 169

Games, 162, 187
Generation, 195

Geography, 110–114, 24, 127
   five themes, 18–19
Gilchrist, Jan Spivey, 152–157
Globe, 51, 62–63, 178
   drawing of, 63
Gold Discovery Day, 142
Gold rush, 84, 202–203
Golden Rule, 30–31
Goods, 266, 276–279, 292, 300
   trading, 294, 316
Government, 24, 42–43
Governor, 24
Graphs
   bar, 306–307, 319
   picture, 280–281, 318, 319
Groups, 22
   putting things into, 164–165
   working together in, 34–35
Gulf, 114

"Happy 4th of July, Jenny Sweeney!" (Kimmelman), 134–137
Heo, Yumi, 308–313
Heroes, 98, 112–115, 138
Hill, 114, 70
History, 28–29, 126–129, 130–133, 158–163, 166–169, 174–175, 211, 226–227, 228–229, 230–231, 234–235, 290
   learning about, 172–173, 228–229
Holidays, 142
Home tools, 190–193

Homes, 74, 151
Hopi Indians, 226
Houses, 74
"How Beetles Became Beautiful" (a Folktale from Brazil), 254–257
Hupa Indians, 231

Icons
  Rosie the Riveter, 290
  Sacagawea, 234–235
Immigrants, 123, 211, 236–241
Imperial Valley (California), 72
Independence Day, 128
Indians, American, see American Indians
International Festival of Masks, 258–259
Internet, R13
Interview, R16
Ireland, 240
Island, 114, 103, 124

Jefferson, Thomas, 29
Jobs, 272–275, 276–279, 282–287, 290–291, 305, 314–315
Johnson, Angela, 86–89
Julia Pfeiffer Burns State Park, 139
Julian, California, 166–169

Key, Francis Scott, 109, R19
Kimmelman, Leslie, 134–137

King High School, 138
King, Martin Luther, Jr., 114, 138, 142, R19

LeBarre, Erika, 104–105
Laird, Addie, 285
Lake, 114
Land, 70–71, 75, 235
  as a resource, 71–75
  on maps, 61, R4–R5, R8–R9, R11
  symbols for, 61
Landmarks, 99, 103, 120, 122–123, 124–125
Language, 212–213, 226, 229, 248
Laws, 3, 19, 44
  and respect, 33
  breaking, 21
  of communities, 18–21
Leaders, 22–25
  of cities, 23
  of communities, 22–25
  of countries, 26
  of schools, 12, 14
  of states, 24
  of the United States, 26, 29, 100
Learning, 158–163
Lewis and Clark, 234–235
Lewis, Captain Meriwether, 234–235
Liberty Bell, 97, 120
Liberty Island, 125
Library, R14–R15
Lincoln Monument 114
Lion and the Mouse, The (Aesop), 38–41
Literature
  "America" (Smith), 104–105

"Children of Long Ago" (Little), 152–157
"Friendship's Rule" (Ford), 8–11
"Happy 4th of July, Jenny Sweeney!" (Kimmelman), 134–137
"How Beetles Became Beautiful" (a Folktale from Brazil), 254–257
Lion and the Mouse, The (Aesop), 38–41
"Making Maps" (Emans), 56–57
One Afternoon (Heo), 308–313
"Quilts": from Cherry Pies and Lullabies (Reiser), 194–201
"Those Building Men" (Johnson), 86–89
"What a Wonderful World" (Weiss and Thiele), 216–219
"Worksong" (Paulsen), 272–275
Little, Lessie Jones, 152–157
Location, 58–61, 62–63
Los Angeles, California, 52

Main idea, 100
"Making Maps" (Emans), 56–57
Mandan Indians, 226
Manufacturing, 267, 270–271, 300–305

Map legend, 68–69, 94, 243, 262
Map symbols, 68–69
Maps, 58–61, 62, 67, 68–69, 95
  find capitals, cities, and states on, 59, R6–R7
  find directions on, 76–77, 95
  follow routes on, 242–243
  locate the four oceans on, 63, R2–R3
  locate the seven continents on, 63, R2–R3
  locate the United States on, 60, R2–R3
  of a neighborhood, 111, 58, 68–69, 94
  of a school, 112–113, 77
  of a zoo, 95
  of American Indian territories, 226–227
  of California, 24, 42, 50, 59, 61, 90, 138, 202, 230, 243, 258, 262, R10–R11
  of the 13 colonies, 127, 131
  of the United States, 60, 236–237, R6–R9
  of the world, 63, R2–R5
  route of Mayflower, 126
  showing land and water on, 61, R4–R5, R8–R9, R11
  symbols on, 68–69, 243, 262
Market, 267, 292–293, 297

Marshall, James, 84, R19
Martin Luther King, Jr., Day, 114
Masks, 258–259
Mayflower (ship), 126
Mayor, 23, 25
Memorial Day, 113
Mexican and Spanish seal, 43
Mexico, 212–213, 240, 252
  Tortillas, 212
Milkman, 190
Miwok Indians, 230
Model, 62, 67
Mohawk Indians, 227
Mojave Desert, 52
Money, 278–279, 295, 296, 297
  earning, 265, 282, 287, 295
  How Money Moves (chart), 295
  saving, 296–297
  spending, 278, 293–294, 295–297, 298–299, 316
  symbol of United States, 120–121
  trading, 294, 297, 316
Monterey County, California, 74
Monuments, 99, 103, 104–105, 114, 122, 123
Moser, Barry, 86–89
Mountain, 114, 70
Mount Rushmore, 99, 104–105, 122–123
Murals, 225
Music, 225, 259
"My Country 'Tis of Thee," 104–105

National Flag Day, 118–119
National holidays, 99, 113–115, 118, 128, 142
National parks
  Point Reyes National Seashore, 90–91
  Redwood National Park, 52
  Yosemite National Park, 52
Nature, caring for, 78–79
Needs, 72–73, 74, 75
Neighborhood, 64–67
  map of, 68–69, 94
New Year's Day, 142
New York Harbor, 123
Nez Perce Indians, 226
Nonfiction, 180–181
North, 76, 95
North America, 63, 126–127, 226
  exploration of, 234–235
  map of, 226–227, R2, R4

Oakland, California, 172
Ocean, 114, 62–63, 71, 240
  Atlantic, 126
  Pacific, 49, 60, 61, R2–R6, R8, R10, R11
Old Spanish Days festival, 187
One Afternoon (Heo), 308–313

Pacific Ocean, 49, 60, 61, R2–R6, R8, R10, R11
Parker, George S., 162, R19
Pasadena, California, 229
Past, 146, 164, 166, 169
Patriotic symbols, 100, 120–121
Patriotism, 99, 110–111, 115
Paulsen, Gary, 272–275
Paulsen, Ruth Wright, 272–275
Peninsula, 114
Philadelphia, Pennsylvania, 131
Physical environment, 52, 55, 70–74, 75, 84, 85, 90–91
Picture graph, 280–281, 318
Pilgrims, 104
Plain, 114
Pledge, 108–109
Pledge of Allegiance, 106–109, 110–111
Poetry
  "Children of Long Ago" (Little), 152–157
  "Friendship's Rule" (Ford), 8–11
  "Happy 4th of July, Jenny Sweeney!" (Kimmelman), 134–137
  "Making Maps" (Emans), 56–57
  "Those Building Men" (Johnson), 86–89
  "Worksong" (Paulsen), 272–275

Points of View, 84–85, 224–225, 290–291
Point Reyes National Seashore, 90–91
Poland, 212–213
  chlodnik, 212
Police Activities League (PAL), 36–37
Police officers, 20, 36–37, 315
Pomo Indians, 226, 230
Pony Express, 175
Potato masher, 190
Present, 146, 165, 167
President, 26, 28, 29, 114, 139
  the first United States, 28–29, 114
Presidents' Day, 114
Principal, 14–15
Problem, 16
Problem solving, 16–17

Q

"Quilts": from Cherry Pies and Lullabies (Reiser), 194–201

R

Radio, 192
Reading Skills
  Categorize and Classify, 52–53
  Cause and Effect, 4–5
  Compare and Contrast, 212–213
  Main Idea and Details, 100–101
  Recall and Retell, 268–269
  Sequence, 148–149
Reagan, Ronald W., 139, R19

Recall, 268–269
Recreation, 83, 84, 238, 239
Redwood National Park, 52
Refrigerator, 190
Reiser, Lynn, 194–201
Religion, 247, 249
  freedom of, 32
Resources, 71–75
  saving, 78–79
  types of, 71
  uses of, 72, 73
Respect, 30–33, 34, 182–183
Responsibility, 13, 15, 33, 234–235
Retell, 268–269
Rights, 32, 33
Rivers, 114, 84, 243
Riverside, California, 138
Rose, 121
Rosie the Riveter, 290
Route, 242–243
Rules, 3, 12, 44
  at school, 12–15, 48
  in a community, 18–21
  of the United States, 129, 133

S

Sacagawea, 234–235, R19
Sacramento, California, 24, 42–43
San Diego, California, 52
San Francisco, California, 37, 243
San Jose, California, 59, 262
Santa Ana, California, 138–139
Santa Barbara, California, 187

Save, 296
Saving money, 296–297
Scarce, 298
Schools
  alike and different, 160–163
  going to, 163
  leaders of, 12, 14
  long ago, 148–149, 158–163
  map of, 112–113, 77
  rules at, 12–15, 48
  today, 159
  tools used in, 160, 161
  workers at, 12, 14, 36
School Resource Officer, 36
Sea, 243
Seasons, 81, 83, 84
Sellers, 277, 278 292–293 294, 297
Sequence, 148–149
Services, 266, 278
  trading, 294, 295, 316
  types of, 278–279, 308–311, 314–315
Settlers, 126, 129, 230–231
  Spanish, 74
Sewing machine, 191
Share, 34, 222
Shelter, 74
Shoshone Indians, 234
Smith, Samuel F., 104–105
Social practices, 210–211, 215, 220–223, 224–225, 226, 228, 229, 230, 231, 238–239, 241, 244–249, 250–253, 258–259
Soil, 71
Solution, 16
Solving problems, 16–17
Songs
  "America" (Smith), 104–105

"What a Wonderful World" (Weiss and Thiele), 216–219
South, 76, 95
Space shuttle, 179
Special times, 250–253
Speech, freedom of, 32
Sportsmanship, 34–35
Spring, 81
Stagebridge (Theater), 172–173
State, 50, 59, 60
  finding on maps, 60, R6–R7
  first in United States, 127
  flag of, 106
  leader of, 24
  parks, 139, 202–203
Statue of Liberty, 103, 105, 123, 124–125
  diagram of, 125
Stores, 277
Stories
  One Afternoon (Heo), 308–313
  "Quilts": from Cherry Pies and Lullabies (Reiser), 194–201
Storytelling, 172–173, 228, 244, 259
Study Skills
  Anticipation Guide, 214–215
  Build Vocabulary, 54–55
  Connect Ideas, 270–271
  Note Taking, 102–103
  Preview and Question, 6–7
  Use Visuals, 150–151
Summer, 81

Symbols, 51, 68, 97–98, 100–101, 120–123
  for land and water on maps, 61
  on maps, 68–69, 243, R2–R11
  of the United States, 97–98, 100, 103, 106–109, 114, 120–123, 124–125, 128–129, 132–133

T

Table, 164–165
Teacher, 12, 25
Technology, 145, 147, 174–179
  change and, 145, 174–179
  for communication, 188–189
  home tools, 151, 190–193
  for transportation, 145, 174–179
Telephone, 188, 192
Television, 193
Theme parks
  Disneyland, 52
  SeaWorld, 52
Thiele, Bob, and George David Weiss, 216–219
Thirteen Colonies, The, 127
"Those Building Men" (Johnson), 86–89
Time line, 29, 79, 111, 147, 170–171, 183, 207, 235, 289
Timucua Indians, 227
Today, 116
Tomorrow, 116
Tools, 145, 160, 163

home, 190–193
long ago, 160, 161, 164–165, 190–193
today, 164–165
Tortillas, 212
Trade, 267, 294, 297, 316
Tradition, 108, 113–115, 118–119, 128, 210, 222, 223, 231, 246, 249, 250–253
Transportation, 75, 163, 174–179
books about, 180–181
of goods, 75
long ago, 163, 174–175, 176, 203
modes of, 75, 85, 174–177, 179
Pony Express, 175
Trees, 71
Trustworthiness, 28–29
Typewriter, 192

Uniforms, 314
Union, 289
United Farm Workers of America, 288, 289
United States of America, the, 60
exploration of, 234–235
first President of, 28–29, 114
first states of, 127
flag of, 98, 106–109, 118–119, 121
history of, 28–29, 109, 126–129, 130–133, 224, 226–227, 228–231, 234–235
law in, 224
leaders of, 26, 28–29, 114, 139
maps of, 60, 131, 226–227, R6–R9

Pledge of Allegiance to, 106–109, 110–111
songs about, 104–105
symbols of, 97–98, 100, 103, 106–109, 114, 120–123, 124–125, 128–129, 132–133
traditions of, 108, 113–115, 118–119, 128, 210, 222, 223, 231
United States Constitution, 29, 100, 129, 133

Valley, 114
Veterans Day, 113
Volunteer, 287
Vote, 3, 7, 26–27

Wants, 298
War, 129
marching drum, 129
Washer, 191
Washington, George, 28–29, 114, 133, R19
Washington Monument, 99, 122
Water
as a resource, 71, 73
on maps, 61, R4–R5, R8–R9, R11
symbols for, 61
types of, 55, 70
uses of, 73
Weather, 80–83
Weaver, Robert C., 224–225
Weiss, George David, and Bob Thiele, 216–219
West, 76, 95

"What a Wonderful World" (Weiss and Thiele), 216–219
Winter, 81
Work, 268, 272–275, 276–279, 283–287, 314–315
inside and outside the home, 186
Workers
children, 285
factory, 285, 301
farm, 289
inside and outside the home, 186
military, 112
Rosie the Riveter, 290
school, 36
strike, 289
union, 289
women, 290
Working together, 16, 34–35
"Worksong" (Paulsen), 272–275
World, 216–219, 236, 241
maps of, 63, R2–R5
songs about, 216–219
World War II, 290

Yesterday, 116
Yosemite National Park, 52

For permission to reprint copyrighted material, grateful acknowledgment is made to the following sources:

Abilene Music: Lyrics from "What a Wonderful World" by George David Weiss and Bob Thiele. Lyrics copyright © 1967 by Range Road Music Inc. and Quartet Music Inc. Lyrics copyright renewed and assigned to Range Road Music Inc., Quartet Music Inc., and Abilene Music.

Atheneum Books for Young Readers, an imprint of Simon & Schuster Children's Publishing Division: Illustrations by Ashley Bryan from *What a Wonderful World* by George David Weiss and Bob Thiele. Illustrations copyright © 1995 by Ashley Bryan.

Chronicle Books LLC, San Francisco, CA: From *Amazing Aircraft* by Seymour Simon. Text copyright © 2002 by Seymour Simon.

Carla Golembe: Illustration by Carla Golembe from *How Night Came from the Sea,* retold by Mary-Joan Gerson. Illustration copyright © 1994 by Carla Golembe.

Groundwood Books Ltd., Canada: Illustrations by Ian Wallace from *The Name of the Tree* by Celia Barker Lottridge. Illustrations copyright © 1989 by Ian Wallace.

Harcourt, Inc.: From *Sometimes* by Keith Baker. Copyright © 1999 by Harcourt, Inc. *Worksong* by Gary Paulsen, illustrated by Ruth Wright Paulsen. Text copyright © 1997 by Gary Paulsen; illustrations copyright © 1997 by Ruth Wright Paulsen.

HarperCollins Publishers: Cover and illustration by Kevin O'Malley from *Chanukah in Chelm* by David A. Adler. Illustrations copyright © 1997 by Kevin O'Malley. From *The Egyptian Cinderella* by Shirley Climo, illustrated by Ruth Heller. Text copyright © 1989 by Shirley Climo; illustrations copyright © 1989 by Ruth Heller. From *The Korean Cinderella* by Shirley Climo, illustrated by Ruth Heller. Text copyright © 1993 by Shirley Climo; illustrations copyright © 1993 by Ruth Heller. "Quilts" from *Cherry Pies and Lullabies* by Lynn Reiser. Copyright © 1998 by Lynn Whisnant Reiser.

Houghton Mifflin Company: Cover illustration by Lois and Louis Darling from *Silent Spring* by Rachel Carson. Illustration copyright © 1962 by Lois and Louis Darling.

Lee & Low Books, Inc., New York, NY 10016: "Children of Long Ago" (Part I and Part II) from *Children of Long Ago* by Lessie Jones Little, illustrated by Jan Spivey Gilchrist. Text copyright © 2000 by Weston W. Little, Sr. Estate; text copyright © 1988 by Weston Little; illustrations copyright © 1988 by Jan Spivey Gilchrist.

Hal Leonard Corporation, on behalf of Quartet Music Inc.: Lyrics from "What a Wonderful World" by George David Weiss and Bob Thiele. Lyrics copyright © 1967 by Range Road Music Inc., Quartet Music Inc., and Abilene Music, Inc. Lyrics copyright renewed and assigned to Range Road Music Inc., Quartet Music Inc., and Abilene Music. International copyright secured.

Little, Brown and Company (Inc.): Cover illustration by Carla Golembe from *How Night Came from the Sea,* retold by Mary-Joan Gerson. Illustration copyright © 1994 by Carla Golembe.

Range Road Music Inc.: Lyrics from "What a Wonderful World" by George David Weiss and Bob Thiele. Lyrics copyright © 1967 by Range Road Music Inc. and Quartet Music Inc. Lyrics copyright renewed and assigned to Range Road Music Inc., Quartet Music Inc., and Abilene Music.

Scholastic Inc.: Cover and illustration from *One Grain of Rice: A Mathematical Folktale* by Demi. Copyright © 1997 by Demi. "Making Maps" by Elaine V. Emans and "Friendship's Rule" by M. Lucille Ford from *Poetry Place Anthology.* Text copyright © 1983 by Edgell Communications. Text and adapted illustrations from *One Afternoon* by Yumi Heo. Copyright © 1994 by Yumi Heo. Published by Orchard Books/Scholastic Inc. From *Those Building Men* by Angela Johnson, illustrated by Barry Moser. Text copyright © 2001 by Angela Johnson; illustrations copyright © 2001 by Barry Moser. Published by the Blue Sky Press/Scholastic Inc.

Albert Whitman & Company: Happy 4th of July, Jenny Sweeney! by Leslie Kimmelman, illustrated by Nancy Cote. Text copyright © 2003 by Leslie Kimmelman; illustrations copyright © 2003 by Nancy Cote.

PHOTO CREDITS GRADE 1 SOCIAL STUDIES

PLACEMENT KEY: (t) top; (b) bottom; (l) left; (r) right; (c) center; (bg) background; (fg) foreground; (i) inset.

COVER: Jon Arnold/DanitaDelimont.com (Sequoia tree)Patty Kenny (Balboa Park); Harcourt (Children).

ENDSHEET IMAGERY: Jon Arnold/DanitaDelimont.com (Sequoia tree); Harcourt (Children); Philip James Corwin/Corbis (Trinidad Lighthouse).

FRONTMATTER: iv-v (bg) Tony Freeman/PhotoEdit; vi-vii (bg) Dwight Ellefson/Superstock; vii (t) Getty Images; ix (t) Leif Skoogfors/Corbis; (br) Tony Freeman/PhotoEdit; x (l) Retrofile.com; (r) Getty Images; xi (bg) Brian A. Vikander/Corbis; (t) Getty Images; xii Bowers Museum of Cultural Art/Corbis; xiii (bg)A. Ramey/PhotoEdit; I2 Gary Conner/PhotoEdit; Corbis; I3 Woodplay of Tampa; I8 Picturequest; Getty Images; I9 Getty Images; Imagestate; I12 Getty Images.

UNIT 1: 1 (t) Zefa Creasource/Masterfile; 2 (b) Bob Daemmrich/The Image Works; (t) Mark Gibson; 3 (tr) David Young-Wolff/PhotoEdit; (tl) Ellen Senisi/The Image Works; (b) Michael Newman/PhotoEdit; 4 Getty Images; 7 Jay LaPrete/AP/Wide World Photos; 13 (tr) Jim Cummins/Getty Images; (bl) Robert Brenner/PhotoEdit; 14 (t) Cindy Charles/PhotoEdit; 15 Tony Freeman/PhotoEdit; 18-19 (bg) Photo Network; 22-23 (bg) Tony Freeman/PhotoEdit; 24 (b) Shmuel Thaler/Index Stock Imagery; 25 (t) Brand X Pictures; (b) Syracuse Newspapers/The Images Works; 28 Francis G. Mayer/Corbis; 29 (b) (tr) Corbis; (tl) The Granger Collection, New York; 31 (b) Jeff Greenberg/PhotoEdit; 32-33 (bg) Jeff Greenberg/The Image Works; 32 (b) David Young-Wolff/PhotoEdit; (t) PictureQuest; 33 (inset) Getty Images; 34 Chris Cole/Getty Images; 36 (b) Kayte M. Deioma/PhotoEdit; 37 AP/Wide World Photos; 42 Bruce Burkhardt/Corbis; (inset) Mark Gibson; 43 (inset) Courtesy of California State Capitol Museum; (tr) Dave G. Houser/Corbis; (tl) Mark Gibson; (c) Nancy Hoyt Belcher; (b) Will Funk/Alpine Aperture.

UNIT 2: 48-49 (t) Mark Gibson; 51 (tr) Felicia Martinez/PhotoEdit; (c) Getty Images; 52 Galen Rowell/Corbis; 59 (t) Mark Gibson; (b) Mike Mullen; 64-65 (bg) Elizabeth Hansen; 65 (inset) Elizabeth Hansen; 66 (inset) Elizabeth Hansen; 70-71 (bg) Craig D. Wood/Panoramic Images; (b) Galen Rowell/Peter Arnold. Inc.; (t) Lester Lefkowitz/Corbis; 71 (br) Dwight Ellefsen/SuperStock; (bl) Jonathan Blair/Corbis; (t) Mark Gibson; 72 (l) Gayle Harper/In-Sight Photography; (r) Joel W. Rogers/Corbis; 72-73 (bg) Ric Ergenbright; 73 (cl) Alan Pitcairn/Grant Heilman Photography; (bl) Dwight Ellefsen/Superstock; (tl) Lester Lefkowitz/Corbis; (br) Neil Rabinowitz/Corbis; (tr) Roy Ooms/Masterfile; (cr) Terres Du Sud/Corbis Sygma; 74 (tl) Chuck Place; 74 (cr)Joseph Sohm/Visions of America, LLC./PictureQuest; (b) Mark Gibson; (tr) Mark Richards/PhotoEdit; (cl) T. Hallstein/Outsight; 75 (c) Alamy Images; (l) Getty Images; 78 Alfred Eisenstaedt/Time Life Pictures/Getty Images; 79 (tl) (b) Alfred Eisenstaedt/Time Life Pictures/Getty Images; (tr) Courtesy of the Lear/Carson Collection Connecticut College; 80 ThinkStock LLC/Getty Images; 80-81 (bg) AP Photo/Jean-Marc Bouju; 81 (bl) Rainbow; (br) Tom Stewart/Corbis; 83 LWA/Corbis; 84 (c) Getty Images; (r) Kevin Dodge/Masterfile; 85 (tl) Alamy Images; (tc) (tr) Getty Images; (b) The Granger Collection, New York; 90 Sarah J.H. Hubbard/Lonely Planet Images; 90-91 (bg) Bill Lies/California Stock Photo; 91 (tr) (c) Galen Rowell/Corbis; (tl) Lee Foster; (b) Alamy.

UNIT 3: 96-97 (t) Index Stock Imagery; 98 (br) NASA; 99 (b) David Young-Wolff/PhotoEdit; (tr) Dennis MacDonald/PhotoEdit; 100 Tom and Pat Leeson; 103 Charles E. Rotkin/Corbis; 109 The Granger Collection, New York; 110 AP/Wide World Photos; 111 Time & Life Pictures/Getty Images; (inset) University of Rochester Library, Rare Books and Special Collections; 112 (t) Dennis MacDonald/PhotoEdit; 112-113 (b) Yogi/Corbis; 113 (cr) Chris Sorensen/Corbis; (cl) Eric A. Clement/U.S. Navy/Getty Images; (t) Morton Beebe/Corbis; 114 (t) Library of Congress; (bl) Philadelphia Museum of Art/Corbis; 115 Getty Images; (inset) Tony Freeman/PhotoEdit; 118

(t) National Flag Day Association; (b) Ozaukee County Historical Society; 119 AP/Las Cruces Sun-News Norm Dettlaff/Wide World Photos; 120 (inset) Alamy Images; Leif Skoogfors/Corbis; 121 (t) Tom and Pat Leeson; 122 (l) Alan Schein Photography/Corbis; (tr) Index Stock Imagery; 123, 124 Alamy Images; 126 Bert Lane/Plimoth Plantation; 127 Nik Wheeler/Corbis; 128 (b) Bettmann/Corbis; 129 Yorktown Victory Center; 130 (b) From the Adams Family Papers Massachusetts Historical Society; (t) The Granger Collection, New York; 131 (inset) Archiving Early America; North Wind Picture Archives; 132 (br) Independence National Historical Park; (t) Lester Lefkowitz/Corbis; (bl) The Granger Collection, New York; 133 (r) Joseph Sohm; ChromoSohm/Corbis; (l) The Granger Collection, New York; 138 Geri Engberg; (inset) Getty Images; 139 (t)(inset) Big Sur Historical Society; (t) Ron Niebrugge/Niebrugge Images; (b) Davis Barber Photography; (b)(inset) Getty Images.

UNIT 4: 144-145 (t) Sean Zwagerman/Ambient Images; 146 (c) Ariel Skelley/Corbis; (t) DeWitt Historical Society/Morton Collection/Getty Images; 147 (cr) Getty Images; (c) Index Stock Imagery; (b) Paul Barton/Corbis; (cl) Ron Kimball/Masterfile; 148 Corbis; 151 (l) Getty Images; (r) Index Stock Imagery; 158 Culver Pictures; 159 (b) Amy Etra/PhotoEdit; (c) Lawrence Migdale; (t) Will Hart/PhotoEdit; 160 (b)(inset) Blackwell History of Education Museum; Jack McConnell/McConnell & McNamara; (t) (inset) The Granger Collection, New York; 161 (bl) (br) Blackwell History of Education Museum; (tr) Gloria Rejune Adams/Old School Square; (tl) The Granger Collection, New York; 162 (t) Bettmann/Corbis; (b) Composite created by Philip Orbanes/Hasbro Games; (c) Hulton-Deutsch Collection/Corbis; 163 (t) Brown Brothers; (b) Dana White/PhotoEdit; 165 9(tcl) (bl) Blackwell History of Education Museum; (tr) Getty Images; (bcr) Gloria Rejune Adams/Old School Square; (tl) The Granger Collection, New York; 166 (bg) Historical Collection Title Insurance and Trust Company San Diego CA; (inset) Jim Whitmer Photography; 167 Elizabeth Hansen; 168 California State Museum; (t) (inset) E.R. Degginger/Color-Pic; 168 (b) (inset) Bruce Coleman, Inc.; 169 (t) Elizabeth Hansen; 170 (br) Amy Etra/PhotoEdit; 172-173 Stagebridge; 174 Michael Schwarz/The Image Works; 175 Brian A. Vikander/Corbis; 176 (b) Brown Brothers; (bc) Culver Pictures; (tc) Hulton/Archive/Getty Images; (t) Museum of Flight/Corbis; 177 (t) Getty Images; John McGrail Photography; (tc) Robert Maust/Photo Agora; (bc) Thomas Mayer/Peter Arnold Inc.; 179 Getty Images; 182 Underwood & Underwood/Corbis; 183 (tl) (inset) Smithsonian Institution; (tr) US Postal Service Licensing Group; 184 (cl) Getty Images; (cr) Corbis; 185 (inset) Retrofile.com; 186 (l) Getty Images; (r) Retrofile.com; 187 (l) Getty Images; (r) Santa Barbara News-Press; 188 Retrofile.com; 190 (bc) Dave L. Ryan/Index Stock Imagery; (bl) (t) Ewing Galloway/Index Stock Imagery; (br) Getty; 191 (bl) Getty Images; (tr) Dave L. Ryan/Index Stock Imagery; (br) (tl) Schenectady Museum; Hall of Electrical History Foundation/Corbis; 192 (b) (c) Hot Ideas/Index Stock Imagery; (t) Superstock; 193 (inset) Bettmann/Corbis; (tr) Getty Images; (tl) Hot Ideas/Index Stock Imagery; (b) Corbis; 202 (fg) Phil Schermeister/Corbis; (b) Robert Holmes; 202-203 (bg)Rick Gerharter/Lonely Planet

Images; 203 (tl) Dave Bartruff/Corbis; (tr) Mark Gibson; (c) Thomas Hallstein/Ambient Images.

UNIT 5: 208-209 (t) Jian Chen/Photo Network; 210 (t) Lee Snider/The Image Works; (c) Getty Images; 211 (t) (c) Bettmann/Corbis; (b) Bob Daemmrich/Stock Boston; (inset) Corbis; 212 StockByte/PictureQuest; 215 Spencer Grant/PhotoEdit; 220 (bg) Michael Newman/PhotoEdit; 221 (bl) Lucine Derhagopian; (tr) Patrick Olear/PhotoEdit; (tl) Zephyr Picture/Index Stock Imagery; 222 (t) Cheryl Richter; 223 Croatian American Cultural Center; 224 (c) BananaStock/PictureQuest; (r) PictureQuest; 225 (tc) (tr) Alamy Images; (b) AP/Wide World Photos; (tl) PictureQuest; 228 Spencer Grant/PhotoEdit; 229 Michael Newman/PhotoEdit; 230 (b) Bowers Museum of Cultural Art/Corbis; (tc) Bruce Farnsworth/Place Stock Photo; (t) Nativestock; (bc) The British Museum/Topham-HIP/The Image Works; 231 Phil Schermeister/Corbis; 234 John Elk III; 235 The Granger Collection, New York; 238 (cl) Bill Aron/PhotoEdit; (b) David Young-Wolff/PhotoEdit; (cr) Gary Conner/PhotoEdit; 239 (b) Adam Woolfitt/Corbis; (tl) Ariel Skelley/Corbis; (inset) Dave Bartruff/Corbis; (tr) Paul Hellander/Danita Delimont Stock Photography; 240 California State Museum; (inset) Corbis; 241 (t) Bob Krist/Corbis; (cr) Richard A. Cooke/Corbis; 250-251 (b) A. Ramey/PhotoEdit; 252 (bg) Jonathan Nourok/PhotoEdit; 253 Robert Brenner/PhotoEdit; 258 Alissa Nicole Creamer; 259 (tr) (tl) (b) Alissa Nicole Creamer; (c) Gary Conner/PhotoEdit.

UNIT 6: 264-265 (t) Peter Bennett/California Stock Photo; 266 (c) Mark Gibson; 267 (b) Bob Donaldson/Pittsburgh Post-Gazette; (t) David Young-Wolff/PhotoEdit; (c) Syracuse Newspapers/Katie Ciccarello/The Image Works; 268 Getty Images; 276 (tl) David Young-Wolff/PhotoEdit; (tr) Ed Young/Corbis; (b) Ron Kimball; 277 (tl) David Young-Wolff/PhotoEdit; (tr) Michael Newman/PhotoEdit; (tc) Roger Ball/Corbis; 278 (t) Bill Aron/PhotoEdit; 279 (tl) Getty Images; (tr) Jonathan Nourok/PhotoEdit; 284 Photophile; 284-285 (bg) John Zoiner; 285 (b) Lewis Wickes Hine/Corbis; 286 (l) Index Stock Imagery; 288 Francisco Rangel/The Image Works; 289 (tr) AP/Wide World Photos; (l) Arthur Schatz/Time Life Pictures/Getty Images; (br) Michael Salas/Time Life Pictures/Getty Images; 290 (r) Alamy Images; 291 (tr) Alamy Images; Corbis; 291 (tl) (tc) Getty Images; (b) The Granger Collection, New York; 292 (r) Lawrence Migdale; 293 (l) Jeff Greenberg/PhotoEdit; 296 David Young-Wolff/PhotoEdit; 299 (tl) Getty Images; 300 (b) Gale Zucker; 300-301 (b) (bg)John Zoiner; (t) (bg) Getty Images; 301 (l) Gale Zucker; (r) Getty Images; 302-304 Gale Zucker; 314 (bl) Jef Zaruba/Corbis; (t) Spencer Grant/The mage Works; (br) Sven Marson/The mage Works; 315 (t) Bob Daemmrich/Stock Boston; (b) Getty Images; (cl) Michael Philip Manheim/The Image Finders; (cr) Rolf Bruderer/Corbis.

All other photos from Harcourt School Library and Photographers: Ken Kinzie; April Riehm and Doug Dukane.

All maps by MAPQUEST.COM.

California
History–Social Science
Standards and
Analysis Skills

Source for California Standards: California Department of Education

History-Social Science Content Standards
A Child's Place in Time and Space

Students in grade one continue a more detailed treatment of the broad concepts of rights and responsibilities in the contemporary world. The classroom serves as a microcosm of society in which decisions are made with respect for individual responsibility, for other people, and for the rules by which we all must live: fair play, good sportsmanship, and respect for the rights and opinions of others. Students examine the geographic and economic aspects of life in their own neighborhoods and compare them to those of people long ago. Students explore the varied backgrounds of American citizens and learn about the symbols, icons, and songs that reflect our common heritage.

1.1 Students describe the rights and individual responsibilities of citizenship.

1.1.1 Understand the rule-making process in a direct democracy (everyone votes on the rules) and in a representative democracy (an elected group of people make the rules), giving examples of both systems in their classroom, school, and community.

1.1.2 Understand the elements of fair play and good sportsmanship, respect for the rights and opinions of others, and respect for rules by which we live, including the meaning of the "Golden Rule."

1.2 Students compare and contrast the absolute and relative locations of places and people and describe the physical and/or human characteristics of places.

1.2.1 Locate on maps and globes their local community, California, the United States, the seven continents, and the four oceans.

1.2.2 Compare the information that can be derived from a three-dimensional model to the information that can be derived from a picture of the same location.

1.2.3 Construct a simple map, using cardinal directions and map symbols.

1.2.4 Describe how location, weather, and physical environment affect the way people live, including the effects on their food, clothing, shelter, transportation, and recreation.

1.3 Students know and understand the symbols, icons, and traditions of the United States that provide continuity and a sense of community across time.

1.3.1 Recite the Pledge of Allegiance and sing songs that express American ideals (e.g., "My Country 'Tis of Thee").

1.3.2 Understand the significance of our national holidays and the heroism and achievements of the people associated with them.

1.3.3 Identify American symbols, landmarks, and essential documents, such as the flag, bald eagle, Statue of Liberty, U.S. Constitution, and Declaration of Independence, and know the people and events associated with them.

1.4 Students compare and contrast everyday life in different times and places around the world and recognize that some aspects of people, places, and things change over time while others stay the same.

1.4.1 Examine the structure of schools and communities in the past.

1.4.2 Study transportation methods of earlier days.

1.4.3 Recognize similarities and differences of earlier generations in such areas as work (inside and outside the home), dress, manners, stories, games, and festivals, drawing from biographies, oral histories, and folklore.

1.5 Students describe the human characteristics of familiar places and the varied backgrounds of American citizens and residents in those places.

1.5.1 Recognize the ways in which they are all part of the same community, sharing principles, goals, and traditions despite their varied ancestry; the forms of diversity in their school and community; and the benefits and challenges of a diverse population.

1.5.2 Understand the ways in which American Indians and immigrants have helped define Californian and American culture.

1.5.3 Compare the beliefs, customs, ceremonies, traditions, and social practices of the varied cultures, drawing from folklore.

1.6 Students understand basic economic concepts and the role of individual choice in a free-market economy.

1.6.1 Understand the concept of exchange and the use of money to purchase goods and services.

1.6.2 Identify the specialized work that people do to manufacture, transport, and market goods and services and the contributions of those who work in the home.

Kindergarten Through Grade Five

History-Social Science Content Standards

Historical and Social Sciences Analysis Skills

The intellectual skills noted below are to be learned through, and applied to, the content standards for kindergarten through grade five. They are to be assessed *only in conjunction with* the content standards in kindergarten through grade five.

In addition to the standards for kindergarten through grade five, students demonstrate the following intellectual, reasoning, reflection, and research skills:

Chronological and Spatial Thinking

1. Students place key events and people of the historical era they are studying in a chronological sequence and within a spatial context; they interpret time lines.

2. Students correctly apply terms related to time, including *past, present, future, decade, century,* and *generation.*

3. Students explain how the present is connected to the past, identifying both similarities and differences between the two, and how some things change over time and some things stay the same.

4. Students use map and globe skills to determine the absolute locations of places and interpret information available through a map's or globe's legend, scale, and symbolic representations.

5. Students judge the significance of the relative location of a place (e.g., proximity to a harbor, on trade routes) and analyze how relative advantages or disadvantages can change over time.

Research, Evidence, and Point of View

1. Students differentiate between primary and secondary sources.

2. Students pose relevant questions about events they encounter in historical documents, eyewitness accounts, oral histories, letters, diaries, artifacts, photographs, maps, artworks, and architecture.

3. Students distinguish fact from fiction by comparing documentary sources on historical figures and events with fictionalized characters and events.

Historical Interpretation

1. Students summarize the key events of the era they are studying and explain the historical contexts of those events.

2. Students identify the human and physical characteristics of the places they are studying and explain how those features form the unique character of those places.

3. Students identify and interpret the multiple causes and effects of historical events.

4. Students conduct cost-benefit analyses of historical and current events.

Trinidad Lighthouse in Trinidad Bay, California